HOW TO ELIMINATE
FEAR
of global economic recession and terrorism
(in three days or less)

by
Wayne Rollan Melton

Fix Bay, Inc., Publishing
P O Box 8184
Reno, NV 89507-8184

Fix Bay, Inc., and its Fix Bay, Inc., Publishing division are a Nevada Corporation.

DESIGNED BY PATTY ATCHESON-MELTON, WOW! DESIGN MARKETING, INC.,
&
MARGIE ENLOW, NuDIRECTIONS GRAPHIC DESIGN MARKETING

Library of Congress info in publication data
2008912047
Melton, Wayne Rollan

1. Self-help 2. Self-improvement 3. Inspirational

ISBN: 978-0-578-00455-6

Contents

Dedicated to my wife, Patty, without whose help and
encouragement this book
never would have been possible.

Acknowledgements

This book never would have reached the marketplace without the diligence, faith and commitment of my wife, Patty Atcheson-Melton. To this day, I remain thankful that a fateful dream awakened Patty, her soul commanding that this book get published.

Her business partner, Margie Enlow of NuDirection Design & Marketing , soon joined the effort by playing a key role creating this project's design and image along with Patty. The public and I each owe these women a debt of gratitude for their talent and perseverance.

When I was just 13 years old, Pulitzer Prize-winning journalist Warren Lerude planted a seed of limitless possibilities, urging me to "always remain curious and inquisitive, and never stop writing in order improve your craft."

Later, during my college years, while I worked a part-time job in Northern Nevada's main library, its director, Martha Gould, instilled the need to read as much as possible about whatever might spark my interest—because doing so would enable me to help others.

Perhaps my greatest inspiration came from Jim Sloan, who served as my personal editor and mentor off and on for more than 15 years. During that process Sloan showed patience in helping me fine-tune and improve my writing skills.

As if an eaglet jettisoned from its nest for the first time, in my mid-40s in 2002 I became a full-time ghostwriter—specializing in books for celebrities, everyday people, businesses and corporations.

Shortly before then, during the summer of 2001, I had worked on occasion on the outskirts of the New York City financial district, as Director of Corporate Communications for Crimsonica, a financial advisement company. I was in my West Coast home office on the fateful morning of the Attack on America.

To his credit, my partner at the time, Robert Mills Sigler, founder, chairman and president of Crimsonica, gave me plenty of encouragement on Sept. 12, 2001, when I told him: "Robert, we're entering a new era, and I'm going to write a book right away on how people can conquer their fear—because these problems will only intensify."

At Robert's insistence, I spent the bulk of the next few months creating the formation of the manuscript you're about to review. By the first week of December 2001, I was able to present the initial manuscript to my terminally ill father as a holiday gift.

Although Robert, Patty and my dad wanted the work published then, something in my soul told me to hold off awhile. Years later, at Patty's insistence, I knew the right time had come to retool the document to incorporate integral information on the world economic crisis.

Soon afterward, as this book's publication time neared, I found myself thinking about the advice given nearly 20 years ago by my friend and spiritual advisor, Phil Bryan, a widely respected gaming industry executive: "Wayne, I can sense that you're a man who carries inspirational messages. You'll know when it's time to bring them to the world."

—Wayne Rollan Melton

Foreword ~ A Message of Hope

A startling dream awakened me in the middle of the night on Nov. 15, 2008. My heart and soul got struck by a revelation, a strong and determined knowledge that my husband, Wayne Rollan Melton, should revive a book manuscript that he had written in the fall of 2001 under his own byline. Back then, only two people other than Wayne had read the initial draft about overcoming fear—me and my husband's late father, my father-in-law, Rollan Melton.

I knew Rollan's opinion carried a lot of weight. In a journalism career of nearly 60 years, Wayne's father had earned the respect of people nationwide as a columnist, published author and newspaper industry executive. The elder Melton had served on the board of directors of Gannett, the nation's largest newspaper group, beside Al Neuharth, founder and publisher of "USA Today."

As a no-holds-barred journalist, Rollan would have told Wayne flat-out if the manuscript was substandard. To my delight, Rollan read the document twice despite his failing health, telling us he found inspiration in the manuscript's insightful recommendations. In December 2001, I swelled with pride when hearing Rollan say: "Wayne, you need to get this published, because it'll help a lot of people."

Although strongly encouraged by Rollan and me at the time, Wayne never sought to get the manuscript published during the year following the Attack on America. Through most of the first decade of this century, from my perspective Wayne seemed to have pretty much forgotten the manuscript.

That changed big-time later on the morning of my life-changing dream, when I spoke to my husband as he cooked oatmeal for his breakfast: "Wayne, you've got to publish that book you wrote about eliminating fear!" I said. "The whole world needs this book—now! This is the time! You need to add details about the current global economic crisis.

This book is amazing, and you need to bring it to people around the globe. Everything in the universe tells me that this should and must happen—now!"

By 10 o'clock that morning, Wayne discovered that the text for the manuscript was irretrievable, within a laptop computer that locked up and permanently jammed in 2004. Eager to find a solution, by noon on the day of my revelation, Wayne discovered the manuscript encrypted at a place online where he had stored it years ago. Then, at my urging, he rewrote and strengthened the initial manuscript, updating details on the world economic crisis and vital information on the re-emerging threat of horrific global terrorism.

"I knew that someday the ideal time would arrive for this book to be introduced to the world," Wayne told me. "And you're right, Patty, the time is now. I wrote this to help lots of people, possibly—I hope—many of them for generations to come."

Then, in December 2008, various ghostwriting commitments and the need to earn a steady personal income forced Wayne to focus his attention on helping his clients' dreams come true. So, at his insistence, I took over all efforts to market and manage the fear book. Along with my business partner, Margie Enlow, I developed this project's image before working in an effort to generate positive publicity and to publish the book.

"Wayne used his keen intuition, extensive journalistic skills and diverse knowledge of history to create what I consider a masterpiece—a work of genius," I told friends. "Although I consider Wayne quite young, he has interviewed tens of thousands of people in his journalistic career, including while an Editor-on-Loan to 'USA Today.'

"Wayne is literally in tune with the positive universe," I say. "Demand for his creativity, research and writing services seems to be steadily increasing as word of his positive reputation spreads."

A former features writer, business writer, entertainment columnist and society columnist, Wayne has researched and interviewed people in diverse situations—everyone from the very poor or homeless to the social elite, including billionaires and top corporate executives. He used these diverse and insightful skills in creating the initial manuscript, which I knew would be a winner the moment I read it for the first time.

As Wayne stresses in this book, from the day Pilgrims first set ground on Plymouth Rock on Dec. 11, 1620, Americans have continually rediscovered the need to overcome great obstacles and challenges. Indeed, discovery and inventions, followed by learning, have been hailed as attributes that help make and keep America great.

From figuring out how to build the Transcontinental Railroad to developing technology that took us to the moon, we've consistently benefited from our abilities to teach, learn and motivate. This time a huge part of our challenge hinges on fear and how to manage its powerful forces.

I'm happy that we're able to bring this message to you here—and that, literally, by overcoming fear, people can enable their dreams to come true if they make their minds up to do just that.

—Patty Atcheson-Melton

CHAPTER ONE

Fear Grips the World

"Osama bin Laden, you can kiss my Royal Irish Ass."

When New York City firefighter Mike Moran blared those words into a microphone, could he have known that cheers would erupt worldwide? Well, to the surprise of many people, that's what happened.

Moran didn't flinch, while thousands of firefighters and police officers erupted in applause. Tens of millions of people watching on TV witnessed pandemonium when Moran's bold words sprang forth at a charity fund-raiser in New York City within a few months after the attack on America, September 11, 2001.

Truly, Moran ignited a raw nerve. International reaction left a lasting impression that many will never forget.

How?

The answer rests in just one word, "Fear." Moran was the first everyday guy to openly and emotionally confront fear of terrorists in a major open public forum—without holding back emotion.

Of course, in the wake of the World Trade Center attack on New York City, there were many brave Americans who responded with courage. Hundreds of firefighters and police officers gave their lives during that morning's rescue effort, as several thousand people perished.

During the days and first several weeks that followed, there were many inspiring speeches by politicians, journalists and everyday folks.

Yet until the minute Moran gave his brief speech in October 2001, only a handful of people even approached such devil-may-care talk in open gatherings. Indeed, it took the courage of this firefighter to break the mold. Moran cracked through that "thing" we call fear to say what he *really* believed.

Yet why did it take someone—anyone—to come forward in such an emotional manner, with a bold tell-it-like-it-is declaration in open public? To some observers, it was as if before that moment Political Correctness had forced us to keep our mouths shut about our understandable anger.

Still, why can't we all express what we honestly feel when times get tough, or stressful in cases where our lives are in danger?

To hear Moran afterward in media interviews, he was merely saying what needed to be exclaimed. Few if any dared blame Moran for choosing blunt words directed at terrorist Osama bin Laden. Moran's brother, Battalion Chief John Moran, had died in the Attack on America.

News Flash: Global Economic Recession Strikes Hard

On the heels of the severe global economic slump in late 2008, as the threat of terrorism continued to loom, the "Washington Post" issued a startling report: "Intelligence officials are warning that the deepening global financial crisis could weaken fragile governments in the world's most dangerous areas."

Worsening matters, the Post said, these factors undermine the ability of the United States and its allies to respond to a new wave of security threats: "U.S. government officials and private analysts say the economic turmoil has heightened the short-term risk of a terrorist attack as radical groups probe for weakening border protections and new gaps in defenses."

"Recession is the new terrorism," Kate Noble, a specialist with the city of Santa Fe, N.M., economic development department told that region's community newspaper.

Millions of jobs across the USA were eliminated during the year, as intense fear gripped the world. How would everyday people from a wide variety of cultures survive?

What would you do to feed yourself and find shelter if you lost your job? Or maybe your home is in foreclosure, or you're desperate for work.

As Barack Obama promised to create 3 million jobs as his presidential administration began, fear continued to grip much of the country. Holiday season spending took a sharp nosedive, consumers terrified of spending money. This lack of spending only served to compound the problem—as fear itself literally worsened the crisis.

Water Cooler Reactions

Seven years earlier, on the morning after Firefighter Moran taunted Osama bin Laden to "kiss my Royal Irish Ass," discussion around water coolers worldwide focused on what Moran had uttered. "Osama bin Laden, you can kiss my Royal Irish Ass" became a battle cry for people everywhere—as folks of various nationalities, skin colors and ethnic backgrounds retooled their words.

Yes, someone finally communicated what common men and women felt, and broke through the fear.

It was as if Moran's bold words pulverized the world's biggest dam. Proverbial waters gushed in the form of endless discussion of this firefighter's heroics, on radio-talk shows, in newspaper columns and among "talking head" TV analysts. All this happened thanks to one man. One voice. One message.

Without saying it directly, Moran was essentially announcing to the world and to Osama bin Laden that "I'm not afraid, or at least I'm dealing with my fears—and I'm going to handle whatever you send my way, and I'll give you something back in return."

Fear Emerged as a Driving Force

"Fear is what is driving everything," Tom Fitzpatrick, chief financial analyst at Citigroup Global Financial Markets Inc., said in November 2008, after treasury yields tumbled to record lows.

Fearing the possible loss of their jobs, 50 sheriff's deputies in Hamilton County, Ohio, attended a public budget hearing as the year ended. A county administrator had recommended that the government cut 201 jobs from the Sheriff's Office due to a revenue shortfall.

In Utah, the Salt Lake Tribune reported that the state's economy was coping with year-over-year job losses. In Maryland, the Baltimore Sun reported that assembly line veterans feared the loss of their longtime jobs if Congress failed to approve a $25 billion rescue plan for the Big Three Automakers.

Similar stories of possible or recent job losses gripped fragile local, regional and national economies worldwide.

On Nov. 22, 2008, the 45th anniversary of the assassination of President John F. Kennedy, Ben Stein wrote in the 'New York Times:' "The Depression (of the 1930s) taught us that if there is enough fear in the economy, lenders will not lend and economic activity will continue indefinitely at a level consistent with serious recession and even depression."

Are You Afraid?

Are you horrified of terrorists and of severe economic recession, which may blossom into The Great Depression II? Are you worried that one of your neighbors might be one of them, preparing to kill you? Do you worry that all stores in your neighborhood will close forever?

The number of questions is almost as numerous as there are solid answers.

- Will terrorists kill us by destroying all the major bridges in the U.S.?

- Will selfish politicians and greedy corporate executives allow the severe recession to worsen, in order to lower stock prices so they can "snatch up" bargains?

- Will *they* fly overhead using crop dusters to spray us with killer pesticides, chemicals or bugs?

- Will *they* smash small planes into nuclear power plants and wipe out millions of people? Will *they* drive giant tractor trailers into major buildings and blow them up with giant bombs?

- Will *they* lay you off from your job, heartlessly carrying out their own ill-intended plan in order to send more jobs overseas?

Oh, yes, and don't forget to ask that big question over and over, without letup—will _they_ use nuclear bombs to blow us all up at once?

And just who are *they* anyway? This brings up scores of additional worrisome questions. Like proverbial gremlins in our clothes driers who steal socks, *they* could be just about anyone. Our neighbors, co-workers, and even friends might end up as possible suspects.

Worst Possible Outcome Envisioned

Jim Cramer, host of CNBC-TV's popular "Mad Money" show warned shortly before Thanksgiving 2008 that the nation's economy would suffer in The Great Depression II—unless the U.S. government provided huge sums of cash to General Motors, as the auto giant faced bankruptcy.

Plus, a growing fear of economic deflation was among factors that pushed the Dow Jones Industrial Average below 8,000, its lowest point in many years.

As the days, weeks and months passed, while the global economic crisis worsened, few people or news reports spoke directly and specifically of a key underlying problem—fear, and how to deal with such emotion.

Sure enough, many people prefer to avoid the mere discussion of fear, partly in order to skirt any worry caused by underlying problems. As comic filmmaker Woody Allen once stated, "It's not that I'm afraid to die, I just don't want to be there when it happens."

Even more succinctly, Lady Nancy Astor, the first woman to serve as a Member of Parliament in the British House of Commons, who died at age 84 in 1964, observed: "The trouble with most people is that they think with their hopes or fears or wishes, rather than with their minds."

Even so, when faced with horrific financial crisis—while also denying the threat of terrorism remains stronger than ever—why did society avoid facing its fears, discussing how to achieve peace of mind? What purpose would such a discussion have served?

To be sure, herein we should heed the advice of African American writer James Arthur Baldwin, an author, playwright, poet and civil rights activist who died in 1987 at age 63: "To defend one's self against fear is simply to ensure that one will, one day, be conquered by it; fears must be faced."

We Could Easily Drive Ourselves Crazy With Questions

There's a train waiting at the railroad station, positioned to pick us all up. It's called The Train of Fear. This locomotive is today's modern speed-train, built in record time on Sept. 11, 2001, without many of us knowing it was even being constructed. The global economic downturn that picked up steam in September 2008 gave more power to this sizable engine.

This rail system travels so fast, in a proverbial sense, that it has far surpassed the Train of Courage, the Train of Survival and even the Train of Faith. This may sound like a harsh analysis, but it's true. There's no denying we have plenty of heroes, courageous citizens. But the fearful are gone from the scene.

You see, more people hopped on the Train of Fear in September 2001 than many of us ever realized at the time. Even to this day, some passengers haven't tried to get off that doomed locomotive. Meanwhile, the Survival and Courage Trains also boast plenty of passengers. But the Fear Train happens to be out in front of the rails, blocking the other engines from making significant progress.

Sure enough, public opinion polls show that huge chunks of Americans still refuse to fly or venture into large crowds.

Many people haven't reverted back to their old habits. In a sense, a number of passengers fell off the Train of Fear out of necessity. On certain occasions, these former riders were forced into other modes of transportation, due to commitments mandated by jobs, families or co-workers. Consider these reformed travelers as the "necessary-brave."

CHAPTER TWO

Where Is the Train of Fear Headed?

The Train of Fear keeps going round-and-round in circles. It's definitely on a certain track, while taking no one where they really need to go!

What's missing from sight, at least in the eyes of many is The Little Train-That-Could, the courageous locomotive that many of us learned about as children. The Train-That-Could pulls the vital core of productivity, inventiveness, and … well, you get the idea.

But now most of us realize analysts and politicians are predicting the War on Terrorism and the War Against Economic Hardship could last many decades, many generations. This sparks worries of what will happen to the economy, which already had dived into recession by late 2001, before rebounding—only to plummet much deeper in 2008.

At the time, economists wondered if huge chunks of our population would curtail spending habits for decades—leaving the economy and growth in a slump for generations. One scenario even has today's U.S. infants doomed to experiencing terror throughout their lives, well into old age if they're lucky enough to live that long.

Could you be another Moran—a True Hero?

Perhaps you wonder what you would have done in the same situation as Mighty Mike Moran. Not only did Moran give his now famous "kiss-my" statement, the firefighter also announced to the world where he lived—as if to dare bin Laden.

Whether we like it or not, fear continues to permeate society. And unless we collectively learn to confront this epidemic and face it head-on, our economy will continue to falter, perhaps for most of the 21st Century. That might sound like a mighty tall statement, far-fetched from some peoples' view.

Whatever you believe, there's no taking away the fact economic harm comes when people stay homebound when it's unnecessary for them to do so. To stay locked in our economic cocoons, hidden from the rest of the world, takes away the very essence of freedoms that we've always enjoyed as Americans.

Don't believe it for a second when someone tells you fear isn't real. Fear is a disease that needs a vaccination. Just as important, fear literally will kill us all if we allow it to spread and permeate.

Why Should We Conquer Fear

Imagine a child who will never go outside due to terror, or a potential mother who will always refuse to have a baby. At any given moment, there are a number of people under such conditions, a small percentage of the world population.

Multiply that many-fold, and we have a desperate situation. With numbers that high, too many potential warriors would already be eliminated. We would be defeated before we even had a chance to fight. We will all die at the hands of terrorism or even from financial worries unless we retaliate with vigor, because our enemy remains relentless. That's a fact. Statement closed. Period.

With that known, why keep hope? Why not embrace fear, and make it our motto? Surely these enemies—terrorism and economic woes—are tireless, and these enemies will not give up until we're destroyed. Just about all of us have seen painfully graphic TV images and newspaper photos of massive numbers of people on the other side of the planet, all screaming for blood—burning our flag. Images of unemployment lines burn the brain.

By letting those images lock us into inaction, we won't be able to make sound decisions. Instead, we should remember that fear has happened to all of us before, in most cases on a much smaller scale. Especially in non-war environments, it's natural and expected in the course of our personal and societal development.

This time the problem intensifies because many of us allow this new fear of terrorism and The Great Depression II to get out of hand and control our lives.

To lesser degrees in the past, before these current crises, fear gripped you often. Maybe it was your first date. Or perhaps that time you didn't want to show your parents your report card. Maybe a physical disease you suffered ignited internal emotional conflict. Or with the knowledge that a loved one was dying, you refused to listen to them and face a "truth."

In all these instances, surely you learned or at least had an opportunity to understand. Maybe you progressed. Maybe you let worries control your reactions, preventing you from reaching maturity.

Each of us is an expert at fear. You're already a fear-pro without necessarily knowing it. The problem is if you're like many people, you've also found yourself unsure how to use those talents during battle conditions here in the "homeland" or within your own "economic household."

You or someone you know is terrified!!!

Such a statement might have sounded significant as the 21st Century began. Now, however, the situation is "real."

Think about it.

Either you or someone you know or have met has decided never to get on a commercial aircraft ever again, or to make a sizable investment of any kind. Either you or someone you know or have met will never go to a public event, or buy another expensive holiday gift.

You or someone you know or have met no longer follows media reports, frightened of what they might discover has happened within the past day.

Consider your acquaintances that are most fearful. You've seen how they've changed. Either it's yourself or someone close. Faced with uncertainty, until now you've known exactly how to help them or yourself despite your hidden inner expertise on how to deal with fear.

Yet if you're confused, you're not alone. Millions have joined your company.

The unknown is a big factor in causing fear and keeping it alive!!

Now that we've got these basics wrapped up, it's time to get down to the nitty-gritty, the definitions and eventually our lessons. In the following pages, you'll learn the inner workings of fear—how to use it, and how to harness its awesome power. We'll investigate ways to react to it and "with" it, and methods of response.

The success or failure of people to grasp these concepts and realities could very well determine our future as a free and vibrant nation. Before we move on, though, let's take a brief moment to acknowledge something we've already alluded to—a "given" that's important to keep in mind throughout these teachings.

NEVER FOR A MOMENT DENY THE FACT THAT THE TERRORIST ENEMIES AND SEVERE ECONOMIC CONDITIONS ARE REAL!! THERE ARE PEOPLE OUT THERE, TERRORISTS IN THIS CASE, WHO WANT YOU DEAD. AND THE DOMESTIC AND INTERNATIONAL ECONOMIES ARE SEVERELY DAMAGED. ALL ALONG THE TERRORISTS WANT TO KILL YOU AS FAST AS THEY CAN, IN WHATEVER METHOD POSSIBLE. THEY WANT YOUR CHILDREN AND YOUR SPOUSE DEAD. THERE IS NO NEGOTIATION WITH THESE PEOPLE—PARTLY BECAUSE THEY HAVE NO FEAR. MEANTIME MILLIONS OF PEOPLE HAVE LOST THEIR JOBS. IF YOU AREN'T ALREADY AMONG THEM, YOU COULD VERY WELL SOON JOIN THEIR RANKS.

As unbelievable as this might sound, in the face of these undeniable truths, fear is a good thing. Three primary challenges involve learning how to harness emotional reaction and then to use it for the betterment of society.

CHAPTER THREE

Learn To Profit Spiritually, Financially and Mentally

You may not remember the time and place, but you have met "terrorists." These people are the bullies of the world. They're brats, they're the creeps who insist on getting their way by danger, intimidation, deceit and other atrocious behaviors.

You probably met your first terrorist in kindergarten, if not before. Undoubtedly, your first terrorist was a jerk, although you may not have known it at the time. He or she tried to take something, or pushed you, or called you horrible names, or said untrue things.

Did that leave you permanently scarred? Probably not, for it's likely that you persevered somehow and carried on with your life. Your parents might have failed to teach you that there are terrorists everywhere, though you learned soon enough.

Some of these jerks were in elementary school. These bullies spread like wildfire in junior high, and in high school they developed new talents of teen-terrorism. If you're old enough, you discovered these "little Napoleons" at your workplace.

Yes, a terrorist is nothing special. You've dealt with him or his kind before, only in the case of Osama bin Laden we're dealing with a guy who is more vicious and hateful than those you've known. This guy is deadly, and he means business.

Other bullies you've known and handled so far meant business, too. Their business is fear. *But unlike the billionaire—bin Laden—they didn't methodically plan to kill millions of people.* **Today's terrorists are warriors, as well as political lobbyists, selfish politicians and greedy corporate executives who sparked this economic crisis.**

Like bin Laden, however, the jerks you've known probably tried to rob you—**spiritually, financially, or mentally.**

- **Spiritually**: Terrorists try to break you down. They try to rip out your heart, the essence of your soul. This is how they think they can control you. **Fear**, creating it and harvesting it, is a big part of their weaponry.

- **Financially**: By "financially," we mean physical possessions— everything from money, to furniture, food or the pennies in your pocket or even the lunch you brought to work or to school today. By creating **fear**, terrorists hope to underpay you, steal from you or catch you off guard.

- **Mentally**: Every terrorist worth his weight in horse poop believes that by breaking you down mentally, he has "won." They know that without your mind, you've probably lost your spirit, your ability to respond.

- **Safety**: Under threat of terrorist attacks, even a person who isn't actually threatened might feel unsafe. Short of actually killing you, this satisfies the terrorists' ultimate goal.

- **Worries**: Threats and fear could increase worries and tensions, distracting people and society from other activities.

- **Productivity**: Intensified fears and using excessive resources to fight terrorism robs society of its productivity. And the word "productivity" in this instance covers many things—from fruitful relationships to output in the workplace.

- **Education**: Some teachers and even college instructors have quickly learned that students and even applicants for teaching positions can find themselves distracted by terrorism and by severe economic conditions.

- **Relationships**: Fear of terrorism and fear of economic hardship threaten personal relationships. Military personnel have been torn away from their families—and killed or injured—due to the War on Terrorism. Some people are even fearful of dating, concerned about falling in love with someone destined to die or get horribly wounded.

Second: To Gain Self-Confidence

In order to win the war on terrorism, and to win the war against economic hardship, it's essential to gain or maintain self-confidence. World leaders have known that to be effective, they must convey an image of being in control or knowledgeable. Terrorist leaders and selfish corporate CEOs that caused our economic crisis seem to know this all too well, just like their despotic predecessors.

When on TV, these warriors, lobbyists, and selfish corporate executives portray themselves as being self-assured, full of knowledge, poise and maturity. Yet what kind of political leaders and overpaid top executives let other people fight wars for them—or work at "slave wages" for them—while the terrorist generals hide in caves and the Wall Street fat cats hide in their mansions?

Are *they* cowards? Are *they* ruled by fear?

That's right!

Yes indeed, at least some terrorists and selfish CEOs might be much more "afraid" than they've tried to project themselves as being. Whether this statement is true or not doesn't matter.

Think of terrorists and overpaid CEOs as mere mice.

All of them are nothing but insignificant bugs.

And remember, insects can be stomped on.

Consider terrorists and selfish Wall Street fat cats in this light, and if you've been afraid you may have found the first step toward self-confidence.

With this in mind, can you think of people who've lost their self confidence as a result of this war or due to the financial crisis? How has this loss affected them and their relationships with you?

If you're already listing more than three people in this category, you're not alone. Here are just some areas of concern:

- **Politics**: Lawmakers who act too confident during this period of economic loss and personal danger risk losing the public's trust. At the same time, those showing less confidence and who appear too cautious risk just as much scorn. Consider the case of former California Governor Gray Davis, who held that office during the Attack on America. When Davis learned the Golden State's bridges were threatened, he decided to tell the public. Some citizens criticized his decision to make the announcement; others were just as vocal, contending that he did the right thing.
- **Travel**: Following the November 2008 attack by terrorists in Mumbai, India, many travel consultants advised people to

avoid traveling to that nation. Others argued that to avoid such excursions merely allows such perpetrators to "win," disrupting vital economic activities.

- **Attack**: On Dec. 3, 2008, a bipartisan panel in Washington, D.C., issued a sweeping report that warns that within five years terrorists likely would use nuclear or biological weapons against the United States. Some analysts urged Americans to take such predictions seriously, while others brushed off the report as nothing but "gloom and doom" or "end-of-the-world" predictions that have been made for thousands of years.
- **Sports**: College football and certain major sporting events were canceled the weekend immediately following Sept. 11. Many folks sharply criticized those decisions, saying we needed to show courage. Others applauded the decisions as marking the right time to mourn.
- **Business**: Wall Street came to a standstill, closed for several business days starting Sept. 11. There were criticisms that the market should have opened sooner, while others praised the use of caution.
- **Airlines**: Championing the need to show self-confidence, the FAA and commercial airline officials agreed to resume flights within a week after 9-11. Months later there were many thousands of airline employees and citizens who still vowed to never fly again. Others complained that such people were overly worried, since there are always risks.

Balance

Because it's the "American way," there will always be people who sharply disagree on what activities society should continue in the face of terrorism and economic struggles. What's essential to remember is that even if we "pull back" on some functions or events, such decisions rarely mean that we're failing to show self-confidence.

Everyone can choose to maintain self-confidence during times of sacrifice, even in the face of war or even joblessness. That age-old saying remains true, "When times get tough, the tough get going." Thus, in order for us to have a healthy balance of fear, we must be **tough**—as individuals, as a society, and as a nation. While under the attack of war and facing job loss or homelessness, it's no time to be wimpy. Being tough means making rough decisions, choices people are likely to criticize. You must be tough if you're going to survive this war and The Great Depression II, and life becomes more difficult than you can imagine now.

This means we must be sure not to start getting into a denial mode. The healthy way to avoid fear doesn't mean denying danger or difficulties, for adopting such an attitude in every instance would be unnecessarily foolish. For example, it would be foolhardy to deny our nation's banking and financial system can be rebuilt and solidified right away.

By continuing to face that problem, financial institutions will be able to at least put themselves back on course to eliminate the type of problems that shattered the economy. And as for terrorism, keep in mind that shortly after the Attack on America, major commercial airlines were able to install bulletproof doors between cabins and cockpits. Public safety has and should remain an urgent concern.

Other areas where it's vital to avoid denial:

Immigration and passports: Keep working to prevent terrorists from entering the USA. Admit there's a security problem due to a lack of proper enforcement of our nation's borders. Refine and strengthen the nation's policy on permitting entrance visas.

Law enforcement: Within a few months after the Attack on America, Congress and the President took initial measures to give police and the FBI "more teeth," necessary to gnaw into terrorism. Yet since then, it has remained essential for our politicians to remain vigilant, adapting quickly to changing needs that undoubtedly will continue to arise.

Water services: Our nation's citizens have reason for concern, because there's no adequate security protecting water systems. Our politicians and utility executives need to face this danger head-on, doing more to implement safety measures.

Food distribution: Here's yet another public service labor stream that's so full of "safety holes" a terrorist could easily broach them, even now—so many years after the Attack on America. Problems must be identified, and plugged fast.

Hospitals and public health system: We all learned quickly that our biological disease detection was inadequate. Officials made plenty of wrong decisions during the initial anthrax attacks early in this century. Rather than denying the problem afterward, authorities should continue to modify, strengthen and improve the system.

Other concerns: There's plenty of other areas where the need to avoid denial remains essential. Affected industries include nuclear power, hotels, restaurants, leisure companies and much more.

CHAPTER FOUR

"The Sky is Falling! The Sky is Falling!"

Remember the old story of Chicken Little, that character who kept running around saying the "Sky is Falling! The Sky is Falling! We're going to tell the king!"

Well, the sky is falling. It has been falling for thousands of years. There's danger everywhere. At every turn, the stars plummet out of the sky. Clouds worldwide continue to crash to Earth, and the continual threat of possible global climate change remains a hot-button topic.

Yet there's a funny thing, though, about Chicken Little. Although he's right that the sky keeps falling, it never has happened to hit Earth. Should we panic, knowing that it'll fall?

There's a danger and real-life threat that terrorism and The Great Depression II have grown more "real" than ever in the mind of the public. We've listed only a handful of potential dangers that could cause panic.

Like we say, it's time for us to be tough. Recognizing the potential for terrorism and for economic hardship doesn't mean we must be afraid.

What it does mean is that, indeed, the sky *is* falling.

Let's face it! There will be more attacks and more economic hardship!!

Well, now that we've established that the sky definitely is falling, it's a good time to convey another reality. No reason for denial here. Simply put, some public officials have clearly told us without question that there will be more terrorist attacks against the USA.

Several times during those first few months initially after the Sept. 11 attack, the FBI issued national warnings. In each case, the public was warned to expect an imminent attack within several days. In each instance, there were no widespread attacks.

To their credit, government leaders and criminal investigators acted in a prudent manner in deciding to issue the warnings. Their decisive actions made it clear that authorities had reason to believe additional threats and worries of more attacks were credible—warnings that have continued on a less consistent basis since then, but remain in force nonetheless.

Put all these factors together and it becomes evident that everyone should do more to respond and to prepare. Every citizen, from lawyers and plumbers to homemakers and school children, must learn to cope during the current crisis.

Third: Regain Vitality at Work, Home and Play

Here's another primary reason to destroy the terrorists' brand of fear: terror—whether caused by warriors or by corporate CEOs and "Wall Street fat cats"—seeks to destroy what it is to be "free." Without freedom we lose ourselves.

Unless we can blast past these challenges, we'll be doomed to a lesser-quality life than our ancestors struggled to create for our generation. Have you ever heard anyone say, "Life is for the living?" If you believe that's the case, you'll understand this is no time to be pussy-footing around big issues.

Let's get personal. Let's achieve. Let's conquer our worries together, as individuals, as groups, as a society and as a nation.

If such a goal means risks are necessary, then so be it. To take risk is to be American, and to be a citizen of the world for that matter. To help people worldwide through this process, we created the 3REST™ System, designed to enable citizens from diverse cultures, faiths, economies and political systems to eliminate fear of global economic recession and terrorism in three days or less.

As you learn how to recognize and manage your individual fears through the 3REST™ system, it'll become clear that taking risks is a big, necessary part of living. Surely, we all take daily risks, a factor that gets microscopic treatment during wartime.

That said, while solidifying and honing your fear-management skills, keep in mind that there are risks you might want to take in the coming weeks, months, and years.

- **Education:** You might need to learn more in order to land another job, either via home schooling or by returning to a formal educational setting.

- **Flying:** Do you want to fly on a commercial aircraft, after refusing to use such a form of travel since Sept. 11, 2001?

- **Events**: Will you want to attend more public events such as concerts and sporting matches, functions you once enjoyed?

- **Economy:** Will you want to spend more of your hard-earned income on luxuries, and resume such spending habits?

- **Relationships:** Will you want to communicate what you've learned here to your spouse, children, friends, associates and others?

Here's a helpful cliché

"You are the master of your own fate."

It's important to keep self-control in focus, when learning how to master and manage fear. Otherwise, it would be too easy to fall back into a pattern of over-worry. Knowing this can help, at a time when you feel most helpless. For instance, even if a rifle is pointed at your car while you're driving down a street, **you're the master of what you can control.**

Bless their souls, those thousands of people who perished during the Attack on America; they could do nothing to save themselves. **Still, all the victims were masters of their own fates—within the environments of what they knew and of what they could control.**

In this light, you will continue to hail as the master of your own fate when it comes to managing and mastering fear. All along, in any environment there'll always be much you don't know, such as what possible attacks are being planned. Rest assured, however, that as you tackle these challenges of identifying and managing your Super Worries, you can remain in control.

- **Decisions**: You'll be in full control, knowing what is the best choice, how to behave in any particular situation.

- **Perspective**: You'll be in full control, in deciding for yourself what potential dangers should cause the most worry.

- **Clarity**: You'll be in full control, realizing that not all of your decisions will have clear-cut, and unbendable answers.

- **Mistakes**: You'll be in full control, knowing "it's human" to make mistakes, that you won't always make the best decisions when it comes to managing your fears.

CHAPTER FIVE

Relax, Just Do It

A man had a chance for the job of his lifetime, a big step in his professional career. On a morning one month after the Attack on America, this fellow was about to take a plane flight to another city in order to take the job interview.

Not long before his scheduled departure, news flashed that an American Airlines jet had crashed in Queens, N.Y. Authorities quickly realized that hundreds of people had been killed.

Fearing the worst, this job candidate decided not to take his scheduled flight. Although his departure and arrival cities were in another part of the USA, he worried that morning's disaster had been the result of a terrorist attack.

So, he chose not to take his flight, and so he missed that morning's interview.

Would you have made a similar decision? Would you have allowed fear or at least serious concern to prevent you from getting the job of your lifetime?

Let's assume this gentleman had made the right decision for himself, for his values, and for his concerns of personal safety. At least he made a decision, targeting what was best for him at the time. What's considered good for one person might not hold true for another. Just as important, he made a choice and lived with his decision, never looking back—or at least so we assume.

In mastering the 3REST™ system of conquering fear, we hope you develop the ability to be "self-aware," knowing who you are and what you want out of life. Remember, we've called this the 3REST™ system because the process enables people to achieve peace of mind in as little as three days.

You'll complete a thorough self-evaluation as a three-day process begins. Questions you'll ask yourself will be numerous and detailed.

You'll need to grasp your own values before making other internal questions, and eventually developing answers.

Motivation: Who am I? What do I want out of life?

Risk: How much of my personal safety, money and peace of mind am I willing to give up in order to pursue certain activities?

Reward: Is what I'm considering worth any risk that I'm willing to take?

Comforts and Pleasures: Is taking certain risks worth achieving and maintaining certain comforts and pleasures I'm striving to achieve—or that I'm accustomed to having?

Just *Who* Is The Enemy, Anyway?

While locked in the heat of war, a natural inclination would be to wonder exactly who it is we're supposed to be afraid of—the enemy who instigated this Attack on America, and subsequently the attack on its economy, for that matter.

When managing fear against an enemy an average guy shouldn't be blamed for wanting to know what his adversaries look like. Even a professional boxer sees his opponent right there in the ring.

Under attack from terrorism, and from greedy corporate fat cats and selfish lobbyists who helped take down our economy, mental images of an "enemy," his name and army aren't clear. To be sure, fuzzy mental pictures come to play, leading to confusion and potentially to more worry and fear.

"I'm afraid, but I don't know who I'm supposed to be afraid of," you might say. "*They* could be anywhere, at any time."

Sure enough, we're told these terrorists are hiding. These evil culprits lurk in things called "cells," or in expensive corporate offices, or in the hearts of misguided politicians, and some of these potential assailants might be intending to attack us with "spores."

We've entered a whole new language, a whole new space, a whole new era. For those of us who are fearful, this only serves to exacerbate what already is a horrifying reality.

Primarily for this reason, tackling fears of terrorists and fears of corporate executives seems like a tricky challenge. Logic dictates that in order to cope with an enemy, one must know him or her. Such conclusions seem reasonable.

We're told one of the primary enemies is Osama bin Laden, who leads armies of terrorists—who supposedly lurk worldwide. And lobbyists stream unfettered in and out of the hallways of Congress most unfettered and supported by huge corporations that move jobs overseas, or eliminate vital regulations on business activities.

All these various forms of "terrorists" lack uniforms. They hide out like cowards waiting to attack us, either with deadly weapons or governmental regulations that pull down the economy. We don't know what these enemies look like. So, we must improvise.

Creative Imagery

Since none of us knows what most of these individual characters look like, a challenging task arises for folks whose fear stems from imagery. At least in the minds of many Americans, life seemingly would be much better if these horrible enemies had faces all of us could easily recognize. At least that way we could find the culprits and attack them.

In a much more clear-cut situation, during World War II we had images of Swastikas and the Nazi flag, Japanese flag, and newsreels. Back then, those enemies were geographically far away from the USA, in fixed locations, and at least we knew what all of them looked like—in distinct uniforms. Other than in instances where spies were involved, Americans had clear-cut images of which armies we were supposed to fear and hate.

Such recognizable factors are lacking from the War on Terrorism and from the War on Corporate Greed amid The Great Depression II, where the enemy thinks he or she is winning because this mysterious aura can create mental tension.

Yet at the onset of learning the 3REST™ system on fighting and conquering fear, you'll discover there's a way to fight back and to cut through the bull. Here's a strategy that won't necessarily be needed by everyone, but some of us can embrace it and have fun—create your own mental images.

That's right, before launching the first phase of the 3REST™ system, get wild with your imagination. Create a mental image, whatever you want, of what these unseen enemies really look like. Later on, this could very well help as you learn to manage fears. Best of all, it's not necessary to be factual.

So, go ahead and allow your imagination to run wild, free and unencumbered. After all, these are enemies that we're talking about, and it's up to us to define them in whatever way we want.

- **Height:** At least one terrorist is about 6 foot 6 inches tall, towering far higher than any of his fellow citizens. Why? He's a bastard, whose mother cheated on her husband by bedding each man from an entire professional football team. How else would we explain the fact he's 18 inches taller than folks in his own country, while towering over virtually all of his "relatives."

- **Transvestites:** The vast majority of today's terrorists—including corporate CEOs, politicians and highly paid lobbyists—are all transvestites. Underneath their everyday street clothes, they wear bras and panties if they're actually men and jock straps if they're actually women. This isn't to say anything bad about everyday transvestites, because at least those people don't make a practice of killing innocent human beings for a living or trashing economies.

- **Losers:** It doesn't matter what any terrorist looks like, whether a warrior or a corporate shill. They're all "losers" anyway. They're losers because they kill, or because they rob you of a job and leave you penniless, because they hate you so much, and because they seemingly lack the ability to love.

In summary, all these various forms of "terrorists" are people that no one will miss when they're dead.

Certainly such graphic images are horrible things to say about anyone. Vivid details chosen for these examples are offensive to some. But war is offensive, and poverty and economic hardship are offensive, and these terrorist clowns were the folks who started it all. And best of all, doesn't it make you feel better, to develop your own creative mental images of these jerks?

The Devil Himself is a Terrorist

Do you believe in the Devil? You know the guy. He's the fellow with the pitchfork, the character you learned about as a child. Even if you're not religious, you know about his character. He's in the movies. He's in some best-selling Stephen King books. He was in a flick called "The Exorcist." And oddly enough, a bit of him, or a lot of him, was in all the various terrorists whom you've personally known throughout life.

The type of terrorists we're worried about today are no different. Some behave as if typical charismatic, self-centered creeps. Bleeding-heart types who insist we must listen to them—including lobbyists—in order to "understand the other side" have got it all wrong. When terrorists kill or eliminate jobs or eliminate regulations on corporations for the sake of greed, they're evil.

That's Devil Stuff.

Pushing aside their hogwash, their mindless reasons for this war, from the American standpoint, all these various people should be told, "You just don't kill innocent people, thousands of them. And you don't just take away the jobs of people nationwide, millions of them. It's against our values. Such violence or such selfishness aimed against the people of our country remains contrary to what we believe as a nation and as a society, and we don't need or want to change what we believe for you, or for anyone else."

When starting a 3REST™ program, keep in mind that this is what most Americans believe. And if you disagree with them, it might be a good idea to embrace your own opinion as you begin.

CHAPTER SIX

Consider Yourself "Part of the Family"

If you feel lonely in your fears of terrorism instigated by warriors, corporations and politicians, remember you're not alone. Millions of Americans feel the same. Taking this "truth" as a positive, remember and embrace that old saying, "there's strength in numbers."

All of us face what officials have described as the real and imminent danger of more terrorist attacks—on our personal safety, our corporate employers, and on our financial systems. When and if such atrocities happen in your neighborhood, state or community, rest assured plenty of other Americans will try to help.

It has been said that Americans are the most giving and caring people in the world. For instance, during the weeks after the Attack on America, partly through charitable events and major donations, residents of the USA contributed more than $1 billion to the victims' families.

"Consider yourself at home," declares the famous copyrighted song from the musical 'Oliver!' "Consider yourself one of the family! We've taken to you so strong, it's clear … we're … going to get along."

Today, as Americans we're "at home" together, unified in facing this issue. Public opinion polls show we're nearly unified, and suddenly locked in a near-100% agreement on a single issue—all forms of terrorism should be taken down.

Not since the beginning of World War II has there been such unification. The depressed and terrified can find at least some sort of comfort in such revelations, knowing none of us is truly alone.

The World's Three Greatest Superpowers!!

Throughout the ages, teachers of the world's greatest and most followed religious beliefs have told of true power. You've undoubtedly heard of these three mighty towers of strength.

Even if you're among the minority of Americans who are agnostic or lack any form of spiritual faith, you may have experienced these sensations. Just about everyone could name them in a flash, for they're **faith, hope and love**. Of course, even the most faithful people know how easy it is for us to forget them. But when we need them, oh brother, we're suddenly the most faithful.

Here's the type of prayer people utter in sudden fear, when they're caught doing something they weren't supposed to—or when an illness hits, or amid other catastrophic situations: *"God, if you'll just let get me through this one thing, this one situation, I promise I'll be good and never do it again. Lord, I have faith you can do this for me!"*

Amazingly, many such prayers come from folks who haven't gone to church in years or who have little spiritual faith. Yet suddenly, when all hope seems lost, they're The World's Most Faithful Believers! Without question, it seems that the heart instinctively knows that "faith can move mountains."

Since the Attack on America, we've seen evidence of this time after time. Remember those folks who were seriously injured, but who pulled through and eventually survived thanks to their willpower. Numerous victims managed to call their homes, despite what they knew would be their imminent deaths.

"Honey, I love you!" such voices blared, leaving messages on home phone message machines. "I'm on an upper floor. The building is burning! A plane hit the tower! I'm going to die, but I want you to know I'll always love you—forever!"

Such statements rush forth in times of stress, with little thought of what's actually being said—for true faith, hope and love have been freed from the soul. Tension and ultimately fears help them spill forth, sometimes in maddening currents that can seem almost uncontrollable and at times even difficult to comprehend.

Man's inhumanity to man gets overshadowed by man's love for his fellow man. Many survivors discovered they were helped in whatever way possible. We saw this passion beaming from the eyes of surviving firefighters, and in the hopeful expressions of tireless rescue workers at ground zero. **Faith! Hope! Love!**

Whether you admit it or not, these attributes are bursting within your heart at this moment! These are truisms that can and will help you when you least expect such assistance, even well after you've mastered the 3REST™ system.

Faith: If you embrace it, it will keep you going, as long as you're alive and willing to allow such power go give guidance.

Hope: Hides in the background. Yet driven by faith, this blessing springs forth when least expected.

Love: Eternally heralded as "the greatest of these," herein rests the answer to solve problems tracked down and captured by faith and hope.

Miracles Do Happen!

More than one month after the World Trade Center crumbled, salvage personnel and firefighters at ground zero heard a sound. Desperate to find the source of the whimper, crews dug through the rubble as fast as possible. Worked to the point of exhaustion, these men and women never halted thanks to their faith.

Driven by hope to continue working, finally, they discovered a paper bag inside what had been a kitchen area of damaged structures. Peering underneath the paper, these rescuers found something no one in his "right mind" would have believed could happen.

Sure enough, there was a cat that had given birth. Several tiny kittens had been suckling at their starved mother's breasts. Bathed by light for the first time, these kitties began to whimper. Help had finally arrived. Officials rushed the animals to a shelter.

It was there that—after giving initial medical attention—workers had the responsibility of naming these four-legged victims. When it came time to name the mother, there was no argument what should be selected—"**Hope**."

Words were unnecessary to describe what just about everyone involved knows happens in life—**miracles happen!** When it seems all hope is lost, such sudden and appreciated blessings happen daily. Even in the heat of crisis, treasures abound.

Consider the story of Josephine Harris, an elderly woman who had been on the 27th Floor of a doomed World Trade Center tower. Concerned firefighters from Chinatown's Latter 6 noticed Josephine's plight and gave assistance.

Port Authority cop David Lim was the first to assist Josephine, who had been in a wheelchair. A firefighter with a giant heart and the strength of a healthy bull, Bill Butler, picked up this frail woman as if saving her had been the entire purpose of his life.

Coaxed by fellow firefighter Tommy Falco, who declared, "Come on, come on Josephine, we have to keep going," she and Company 6 made it down safely to the stairwell's fourth floor. It was there that this tired woman declared that it was time to stop.

Realizing she was over-tired, the firefighters obliged. Momentarily, the building collapsed around them. But somehow that one small section of the Fourth Floor stairwell where they stood remained intact. And thanks to Josephine's declaration to stop in that precise spot, these brave men of Company 6 survived.

If they had stopped on a floor above, they'd be dead. Below, the fates would have been similar. In that horrible moment, thousands of people died all around them. After being blanketed in darkness the first several minutes, Company 6 finally saw a beam of light!

Among the "lucky" ones, from that moment forward these unforgettable firefighters called Josephine Harris "our angel." Each of these survivors discovered what he has always known, that **miracles happen**.

When mastering the 3REST™ system during a short three days, a sense that gifts spring forth everywhere becomes evident. To be alive is to know that good things can and do happen daily.

Sometimes, everyday entertainment sources bring this message home time and time again. Perhaps one of the greatest such messages sprang forth in the smash 1993 movie about dinosaurs starring Jeff Goldblum, Sam Neill and Laura Dern, "Jurassic Park."

After studying a pre-historic species, the film's humans surmised: "Life finds a way." Such basic, common sense remained evident in the wake of the Attack on America and in countless stories of how some U.S. soldiers survived battles in Iraq in a round of real-life miracles, when indeed we all discovered that "Life finds a way."

And just like when Dorothy from Kansas utters when her dreams from Over the Rainbow ended, "There's no place like home."

In learning to master fear, your personal values come to play. Unless we have values of some kind, from social preferences to foods considered favorites or acceptable, we're simply not living.

Thus, if we value fear most, we'll embrace fear. If we value freedom most, we'll embrace freedom.

Yet these two characteristics rarely mix well, for fear and freedom are like the positive and negative ends of a magnet that refuse to join each other. And so it is that by using your values of hope, faith and love—or without them, depending on what your values dictate—you'll have a decision to make.

What will you decide?

Will you choose to embrace fear?

"If I Had No Bad Luck, I'd Have No Luck At All"

OK, miracles happen.

But that doesn't mean we should deny horrible things occur.

For much of the 1960s during the Vietnam War, and well in to the 1970s, millions of people worldwide made fun of their own fears.

Both city folks and country folks laughed heartily during the TV comedy hoedown "Hee Haw!"

Much of this oddball show's best humor featured weekly skits focused on the fact that bad things happen. Some tragedies will *occur no matter what we do to prevent them.*

"Gloom, despair and agony on me!" colorful Hee Haw characters wailed, led by musical talents Roy Clark and the late Buck Owens. Many viewers awaited each show with much anticipation.

 Others shunned the program as if it were the stupidest entertainment anywhere. For these disheartened souls, "gloom-despair" skits were a full distraction.

Whatever the case, there's no denying many people enjoyed making fun of fear—along with its age-old friend, Bad Luck.

"Ah, there's no way to escape treachery," some people contend. "When your time is up, your time is up. There's no way to fight the Grim Reaper. There's no reason to count your blessings before they hatch … After all, there's only two guarantees in life—death and taxes."

Like we say, bad things happen. Bad things will happen to you in your life! Bad things have always happened to you, and for that matter, you should remember tragedies occur for everyone you've known or will ever know. Also face the fact and realize—take a deep breath for a moment and know it's true—someday you will die.

Yes, we're diving into a bold part where there's no reason for denial. So, say it out loud, now, this very moment—before your thoughts have time to skip to something else.

"Someday, I will die!"

It's true, of course.

So, are you going to run outside now in panic, telling yourself and everyone you come into contact with that it's going to happen?

Well, if you're reading this rather than high-tailing it down the street, then odds are good that you've faced the notion of your own eventual death before. You've thought about your own eventual "demise," the fact that someday you're going to leave this worldly planet.

Odds are better than merely excellent that in some way, somehow in your past you've pondered this eventual event. In whatever way you could, you've managed to cope. Perhaps you accomplished this by getting into a regular phase of denial. Or maybe you've joined a church or a religion to get guidance.

Many people rely on hope and faith, whether they realize it or not. Hope reigns eternal that they'll never die. Faith tells them that somehow scientists will discover a miracle drug that results in physical eternity for us all.

Still, there's no denying the fact that someday you and they will die. **And there's a chance that you might even die or go into poverty or become jobless or homeless at the hands of terrorists—either from those warriors or from the corporate elite.**

Just as titillating, there's a chance you'll win a million-dollar lottery, or suddenly learn to speak seven languages or that your children will grow up to invent a cure for cancer.

All these scenarios, of course, are "numbers games." Still, there's no question that "bad" things have happened to you, and that more "bad" things will happen in your lifetime. In the minds of many, "life is nothing but a bucket of tears." Among indisputable examples:

- **Pain**: You've suffered physical pain in the past, and it's likely that you'll have to undergo plenty of more pain before you perish.

- **Loss**: Everyone you know will die, even your children and your parents. If you're "lucky" enough to reach 100 years old, more than 99.8% of the people you knew as a child will be gone.

- **Taxes**: That never-lost cliché reaches into your pocketbook, robbing you of cash you could have spent on other things.

- **Murder**: While you're alive, millions of people worldwide will be slain in everything from wars to common robberies. As long as you're alive, there's a chance you'll become one of these victims.

- **Obscurity**: If you're not a U.S. president or celebrity, the vast majority of your fellow humans will never know you, or that you ever existed. Unless recognized by future generations, odds are overwhelming that after death you'll never be missed by much of anyone other than your family and friends.

When will your next personal horrors occur? Will it be tonight, tomorrow or next week? You know something terrible will happen, but where and when?

By this point in life, since you're old enough to read, you've come to realize more pain will come. And, whether you realize it or not, you've developed a keen sense of how to manage fear.

Even if you're terrified at the mere sound of a commercial airliner, fear management already is part of your make-up. If your hair stands on end at the mere thought of flying, that's how you've decided to react.

Instinctively, or knowingly, you're making decisions.

Consider the actual terrorists, whether they're warriors, corporate giants, lawyers or lobbyists. Are terrorists filled with fear, the moment before they kill or terminate the "innocents" in horrible acts of violence or via corporate greed? Well, perhaps some terrorists are horrified, trembling in their own final moments. Yet from what we've learned, from what terrorism experts have proclaimed, these evil-minded individuals aren't afraid in the least!

Why? Are you afraid, numbed with fear while terrorists are willing to die, rob or deregulate Corporate America without a second thought? Are the terrorists better than you somehow, because they're unafraid while you're petrified?

Certainly, you're just as strong-minded as them, just as smart, just as human, and filled with many similar, natural tendencies.

The difference between you and terrorists—including corporate lobbyists and selfish politicians—is that *they have decided not to be afraid! You, on the other hand, have decided to be afraid!*

Please stop here for a second and think about this for a moment. Terrorists are making decisions, and they've trained their minds to be different than yours—to show no fear amid their dastardly acts.

Some condemned killers go to the electric chair horrified, soiling their pants. Other killers show little emotion in their final moments before execution, their low heartbeats proving relative indifference.

This is not to imply, of course, that you're condemned to die or to become impoverished at the hands of terrorists. What should remain clear is that you can train your mind; you can teach yourself to respond with certain behaviors.

If fear is your choice, that's OK within the framework of your personal desires. Conversely, the opposite of fear might tend to help bring you more peace of mind.

"Listen My Children, And You Shall Hear…"

As children in grade school, we learned of heroic Paul Revere and his midnight ride to warn patriots that the British were coming.

Crude though the manner seems today, Revere rode by horseback through the countryside—from town to town—to spread his cry of alarm. Driven by a yearning for freedom rather than fear, Revere gave his fellow colonists time to react and to respond.

Imagine a similar emergency warning system today. Envision a New York City resident on Sept. 11, 2001, racing by horseback to New Jersey to tell everyone that "the terrorists are coming!"

Even under a Pony Express-style system with horse-riding messengers passing word of the war to one another, it would take nearly three days for the news to reach the West Coast.

Under that scenario, folks in California wouldn't have started being "afraid" until at least Sept. 14. That's because they wouldn't have known *they **had** to be afraid*.

Today's lightning-fast technology enables all of us to know through our initial shock when it's "time to be afraid." So, immediately after the Attack on America, pity those poor West Coasters in the U.S. because they "needed" to start being afraid sooner than would have been necessary in Revere's day.

During subsequent weeks after the Attack on America, thanks partly to rapid-fire news reports, mail recipients were convinced they "needed" to be terrified. Depending on our individual circumstances, some of us chose to be afraid to drink water from public utilities.

Through that period, and ever since, the thinking has been, some Americans seem to encourage fear by telling others they're terrified. Essentially, these people are saying:

Security: We must be afraid, because they're going to get us, so let's buy all the tents and gas masks we can!

Travel: We need to be afraid of traveling, because if we try any mode of transportation they might get us.

Crowds: We need to avoid large crowds for the rest of our lives, because any major public event is a potential target.

Money: We need to be afraid to spend a dime, because if all the banks blow up or if the economy bombs, our life savings will disappear.

Heralded as the Need-Fear Gang, these folks were infected with a newly discovered disease, for all intents and purposes. These people aren't weak, or losers, or typical cowards by any stretch of the imagination. It's just that the Need-Fear Gang collectively decided that the sky was falling, and that bad things result in the worst possible consequences.

Thankfully, however, a majority of those from the Need-Fear Gang are still alive today. Are you among them?

Hopefully, you're just like 99% of your comrades who are doing just fine, indeed. While we await the next attacks, though, like many Need-Fear Gang members, you might find yourself rigid—locked with so much fear that it's impossible to function the way you did before the Twin Tower Disaster and The Great Depression II.

Anyway, our condolences go out to you Need-Fear Gang members, heartfelt messages sent from those of us who realize you're only human and there's absolutely nothing wrong with you for joining the Need-Fear Gang. Joining them just happens to be a decision you made. Surely, entering the gang was the right choice for you, since you're doing just fine physically—or at least odds seem great that you're at least in average-to-good health.

Oh, and by the way, have you met anyone from the Hardly Fearful Crowd? People within this segment of our population, millions upon millions of them, spend money with little worry, go to baseball and football games in huge stadiums, and some of them even fly in commercial airliners.

And many of those who lost their jobs continue their relentless search for employment, hopeful for a positive change—or they've joined the growing ranks of the self-employed, learning through perseverance to earn incomes from home via the Internet.

This is not to imply that Hardly Fearful Crowd members are cheap, or that they think they're better than Need-Fear Gang members. Without question, people from these separate segments of our society are— overall—no better or worse than each other.

Similarities & Differences

Nonetheless, Need-Fear Gang members surely must envy those in the Hardly Fearful crowd—since people with fewer worries seem to get better sleep at night.

If you're a member of the Need-Fear Gang, do you envy those who get to sleep in on Sunday mornings, while you're up at the crack of dawn, busy worrying about what *could* happen? Are you angry, because Hardly Fearful folks refuse to worry the way you decided to do?

All along, public opinion polls signify our nation is suddenly unified at near-unanimous agreement on a single issue. Our fight against terrorism has glued everyone together, although there remain differences on how to wage these battles and even about who the real terrorists actually are.

Still, no one seems to acknowledge that America is suddenly cracked, seemingly down the middle. We're vastly unified on some issues by outward appearances, but we're sharply divided within our hearts.

How to Eliminate Fear

In the wake of electing Barack Obama as our first African American U.S. President, some citizens are fearful, worried that he lacks sufficient experience and knowledge—while tens of millions of optimistic voters feel otherwise.

Chunks of our population have jumped into the Need-Fear Gang, while others still prefer Hardly Fearful.

When more battles erupt, both economically and on the war front, which of these factions do you think will better serve and protect America?

Would the Need-Fear Gang lead the way toward resounding victory, defeating the enemy around every corner—or would the Hardly Fearful Folks get the job done best?

As you form your opinions in this regard, while honing fear management skills, it might be helpful to remember Paul Revere.

According to legend, during the midnight ride he was Hardly Fearful.

For, borne on the night-wind of the Past
Through all our history, to the last
In the hour of darkness and peril and need
The people will waken and listen to hear
The horrifying hoof-beat of that steed
And the midnight message of Paul Revere
-Henry Wadsworth Longfellow, 1860

One of These Days, Oh One of These Days!!

Pity poor Ralph Cramden.

Played by the late Jackie Gleason in the hit 1950s TV sitcom "The Honeymooners," Ralph got frustrated when he didn't have his way. Ralph wanted to be "The Man," but his wife, Alice, ruled.

"One of these days, Alice, one of these days!" Ralph would declare, in what seemed to be just about every episode. "Pow, Right in the kisser!"

Marking that exclamation, self-assured and over-confident Ralph would smash his fist into the air—hitting no one.

Audiences roared in laughter each time Ralph went into such tirades, even if they had seen him behave this way many times.

Ralph came off as lovable because he was just that, full of love and devotion despite his bumbling behavior. Continual frustration stemmed from the fact Ralph *always wanted to be a hero but lacked guts to carry through with his plans.*

Coupled with this was something unspoken, something powerful—a motivating tension called fear. Usually this involved fear of not being loved, of not being a success, of being found out as a fool, and fear of eventual loss of some sort.

Of course, no one ever expressed Ralph's predicaments on these terms, openly describing the problem. That's how life works.

Perhaps most of all, Ralph feared losing Alice, of being unable to achieve his undying goal to win her admiration as a Hero.

Well, like it or not, these days millions of Need-Fear Gang members across the USA are Ralph Cramdens. Such people are afraid of losing their loved ones, of losing the younger generation to war, of taking any kind of substantial risk in order to gain their freedom.

Certainly, Ralph was far from intellectual, and these days, both the educated and uneducated within the Need-Fear Gang are like him. This roly-poly character made his living toiling as a bus driver. Today's Ralphs are in every profession imaginable. You might even be a Ralph Cramden without knowing it.

Here's a way to know: Do you love your family? Do you want to be a success at something, to take risks? Do you make mistakes, and sometimes—more often than not—get "caught" for your missteps. Throughout all this, deep down, do you think you're overly afraid of terrorism and of the faltering economy, beyond the point of what's reasonable?

And like Ralph, do you always eventually quit struggling for success before reaching your big goals due to fear?

Answer "yes" because of how terrorists and greedy corporations hit your psyche, and that means you're a Ralph Cramden.

What are you going to do about it?

What will you decide?

CHAPTER SEVEN

Graveyards Are Full Of People
Who Were "Fearless!!!"

The first four Americans to die in U.S. military operations in the War on Terrorism were heralded as fearless, brave soldiers who loved their country. Showing no fear failed to save these men.

None died in combat. Two Army soldiers were killed in a crash of a search-and-rescue helicopter in Pakistan. An American airman died from injuries suffered in a forklift vehicle accident in the region. The fourth victim, 20-year-old Machinist's Mate Fireman Apprentice Bryant Davis, fell from the USS Kitty Hawk.

Besides the thousands already killed in Iraq and Afghanistan, through the course of the War on Terrorism more U.S. military men and women will perish. Like the first four, future combat fatalities will have been heralded as fearless and brave.

Each soldier, sailor and flyer whose body is found shall return home in a casket, draped with an American flag. Other than those who are cremated, their bodies will help fill graveyards, many of them already packed with countless thousands of other U.S. military personnel that gave their lives for our country.

A lack of fear, or at least an ability to repress it during times of terrible struggle, will have done nothing to save them. In passing, they will have joined everyday, common U.S. citizens who died during the first hours of this war.

Each year, millions of Americans visit Arlington National Cemetery outside Washington, D.C. National heroes laid to rest there include President John F. Kennedy, struck by an assassin's bullet in November 1963—heralded as a pivotal change in American history.

Author of the best-selling 1950s book "Profiles in Courage," Kennedy rests near the heart of the cemetery. The eternal flame at JFK's headstone celebrates bravery, yet it is partly the ability to show such strength that got him and most of those poor soldiers near him under Arlington's grass.

On May 13, 1864, Pvt. William Henry Christman of the 67th Pennsylvania Infantry became the first U.S. military serviceman interred at Arlington. A seemingly unending line of war dead followed. U.S. military veterans buried there include Medal of Honor Winner Audie Murphy, who single-handedly killed 50 Germans on Jan. 26, 1945—nearly a generation before he died in a plane crash.

Did these men and women die so you could be afraid today? Would they want you to be terrified, gripped in fear and unable to function?

Whether they were drafted against their will or gladly signed into the military, these soldiers knew they faced a danger of death.

Many of you are children, grandchildren and great-grandchildren of these war dead. The circle of destruction widens when we realize non-military personnel have joined their ranks. Those thousands who died in the Pennsylvania field, at the Pentagon, and at the World Trade Center, including hundreds of New York firefighters and police officers, are rightfully enshrined in our memories as heroes.

Many of these same victims were alive in the early 1960s, youngsters when they heard radio broadcasts or saw TV images of civil rights leader, the Rev. Dr. Martin Luther King Jr., give his famous "I have a dream" speech. That ageless public address at the Lincoln Memorial not far from Arlington still echoes today. More than merely a vocal expression of hope for racial equality, that speech brought home the importance of having vision.

Heaven knows most of those who died Sept. 11, 2001, had dreams of their own.

If the ghosts of all these citizens and soldiers were to rise today, their spirits wouldn't march into your bedroom and ask you to be afraid. JFK's brother, Joseph Kennedy Jr., a pilot shot down in action during World War II, wouldn't beg you to show senseless fear.

And President Abraham Lincoln, killed by an assassin after the president had a premonition-dream that his killing would happen, surely would have answers filled with wisdom—none recommending you become frightful at every moment.

Without question, even if the ghosts do not exist, these deceased Americans are with us all at every moment. Their spirits are with us as we watch the horrors of war on TV. Their spirits are with us as we weep for our departed loved ones, for those killed in burning buildings and by falling rubble—or in nations on the other side of the globe.

Fear—it's such a little word, a miniscule word, and a senseless word; it's small and insignificant when compared to the message our heroes gave us in sacrificing their lives. Fear is what they lost in giving up their lives, leaving us to make our own choices.

So, perhaps you'll decide to keep them in mind as you learn to manage your own worries of terrorism and financial crisis. Trust what your heart tells you about these heroes' wishes for you. And once again keep in mind those first four caskets that returned to the USA from this war—with more caskets to follow in the months and years to come.

The Ultimate Nightmare

Stress symptoms gripped a whopping 90% of Americans in the five days after the Sept. 11, 2001, attacks. Angry outbursts, nightmares, and other significant signs of emotional stress walloped people from coast-to-coast.

Worse than a mere epidemic, this far-reaching psychological impact was quickly described as a "pandemic" by at least one researcher familiar with a Rand Research Institute poll.

A sudden, unwanted wakeup call aroused a nation that had been repeatedly warned by experts that an attack would someday occur. Once that deadly strike happened, anger, rage and fear spread like fire whipped by a 100-mile-per-hour wind.

Many mothers, particularly in the Northeast, wept throughout the night of the first several attacks. All eyes glued to TV sets, many unable to pull away more than a few hours daily. Stores emptied as if everyone on the planet had "beamed up" to a Star Trek spaceship.

Stunned, shocked and in disbelief, many Americans reacted as if members of their families were killed or wounded, even if they didn't personally know victims. To say perspectives had changed would be a bit of an understatement.

Like any day in the USA, numerous citizens chose to kill themselves on Sept. 11. But non-terrorist suicides seemed to take on a new meaning. Anxiety shot through the hearts of children, ripped the minds of mature adults, and left politicians stunned.

Sensations of helplessness raced through the bloodstreams of even tough Americans, from athletes to cops and top-level executives. Especially in those first several days, plenty of big-name celebrities were nowhere to be seen in public. Skies emptied of commercial aircraft. Financial markets stayed closed.

"Even people far from the attacks sites showed stress symptoms," Dr. Mark Schuster told one reporter. After leading a Rand Institute study, Schuster concluded that the country as a whole had reacted to the attacks personally.

Such polls proved unnecessary for Americans to realize what they already knew. When people finally ventured into supermarkets, restaurants and general merchandise stores to get the necessities of life, almost all they heard was talk of the attacks.

There had been no time for solemn analysis of the nation's war dead, or what they would have wanted. Any thought-provoking, in-depth discussion of how to cope with fear seemed impossible.

Too much information overwhelmed the senses rapid-fire, making it difficult for the average psyche to make sense of what happened. Shock. Disbelief. Horror. Rage, and perhaps most of all—fear.

Results of this Rand poll published in the "New England Journal of Medicine" concluded that people had angry outbursts, couldn't concentrate, and found trouble falling asleep or staying asleep. Any reminder of that event often sparked additional upset.

Unable to ignore the psychological impact on America, politicians strived to convey their message that everything remained in control. Yet many people sensed mixed messages, actions and inactions that only served to increase anxieties.

Stressful Symptoms Abound

During the days following the Attack on America, nearly half of children feared for their personal safety, as parents fretted over how to communicate with their youngsters. Those especially stressed included women and minorities.

In issuing its official findings, Rand warned Americans "that psychological effects of the recent terrorism attacks are unlikely to disappear soon."

Its research team noted ongoing terrorist threats and attacks were likely to continue as stress factors. As a result, clinicians were warned to anticipate that even people far from any future attacks may have trauma-related symptoms of stress.

On the positive side, the report said, some Americans found or developed their own ways to cope. Taking this a step further, those same findings remain useful today amid the continued threat of terrorist attacks in warfare and on our economy:

- **Talking**: Ninety-eight percent talked with others about their thoughts or feelings.

- **Religion**: Ninety percent turned to their spiritual beliefs.

- **Groups**: Sixty percent joined group activities such as discussions and vigils.

- **Media**: Thirty-nine percent avoided TV and other reminders.

- **Charity**: Thirty-six percent donated money or blood.

In many ways, individually and collectively Americans reacted as if they would behave in any "everyday" tragedy within their own families—only in this case the impact was far wider and all encompassing in image and impact.

Shock and sensations of numbness were followed by fear, sadness and ultimately action. Needless to say, terrorism proved again that it's perhaps the King of All Stress Givers.

Except for an all-out war on the streets of America, in the minds of some people only a nuclear bomb flying in a missile toward the USA or a moon-sized meteor streaming toward Earth could have possibly caused such a terror.

Yet a major positive remained. Stung by unwanted reality, our nation had a chance to "circle the psychological wagons" so to speak. This War on Terrorism brings home the reality that there is time for each of us to learn about fear and how to manage it for our benefit.

From the day Pilgrims first set ground on Plymouth Rock on Dec. 11, 1620, Americans have continually rediscovered the need to learn to overcome great obstacles and challenges. Indeed, discovery and inventions, followed by learning, have been hailed as attributes that help make and keep America great.

From figuring out how to build the Transcontinental Railroad to developing technology that took us to the moon, we've consistently benefited from our abilities to teach, learn and motivate. This time a huge part of our challenge hinges on fear and how to manage its powerful forces.

Lucky for us, no major new tests are necessary to begin this journey, for intricacies of fear are already known. Blessed by this revelation, let's relax and learn.

Like they say, "Knowledge is power," and once you have it you'll be able to act instinctively *in whatever way you choose. Like a black belt in karate or a seasoned yoga expert, you're on the verge of becoming a master of fear. Before long, you will be holding up a badge within your soul, a shield emblazoned with the words "I am in control."*

History Remains on Your Side

Whether they were fearful or brave, none of the 6 million Jews slaughtered by Adolph Hitler's Third Reich deserved to die. Courageous and timid people were sent to their deaths in gas-filled execution chambers, men, women and children.

Joan of Arc had more faith and courage than many men, but that failed to prevent her from getting burned at the stake.

Still, when a person allows fear to take control, he or she ceases to function in everyday life. An easy way to "lose" is for us to allow ourselves to be beaten into submission, whether the enemy is the environment, or scientific advances not yet made, or terrorists.

When the Wright Brothers took the first successful plane flights at Kitty Hawk, N.C., on Dec. 17, 1903, common sense might have dictated that they would die. Many "brave" men had tried similar efforts, only to learn all too late that gravity "wins and kills."

Still, the Wright Brothers remained convinced success was possible. Their pre-testing and gliding work beforehand helped provide motivation.

Perhaps to Orville Wright and Wilbur Wright everything came down to a "numbers game," where the odds were in their favor. Humanity's ageless dream of flight became reality, as Orville and Wilbur each stared potential fear in the face and pushed the throttle hard during separate flights.

For all the Wright Brothers' efforts, surveys during the months following the Attack on America showed that 10 percent of Americans had started refusing to fly.

All along, news reports indicated that the odds of getting killed in a commercial jet crash are so great that a person would have to fly every day for 15,000 years before getting killed in such a mishap.

Tell this to surviving relatives of victims and to those injured who miraculously survived, and maybe you'd get stern looks. Such scorn would not erase the fact that to a great degree, the decision to "be afraid" is a numbers game.

Fear Itself is a "Numbers Game"

Before deciding whether to be terrified in advance of a certain event, a potential warrior ponders life's fateful Roulette Wheel. Everything comes down to perceived "odds," chances a plane will crash, a terrorist will attack, the economy will crumble, or that a nuclear attack will strike.

Many innovators renowned for their great abilities sometimes discover too late that they were "wrong." They either didn't worry enough, or should have fretted more over potential outcomes.

Some leaders of the former Czechoslovakia believed Hitler's promise that he would never attack, until the day Nazi tanks cruised into their nation. World-renowned escape artist Harry Houdini might have thought himself invincible, but as far as anyone knows he wasn't able to escape the grave.

Japanese warriors caught U.S. sailors off guard at Pearl Harbor on Dec. 7, 1941, as many American military personnel believed the odds of such an attack were astronomical.

Fictional characters also portray important lessons about fear. In the smash 1988 film "Rainman," Dustin Hoffman portrayed an idiot savant with unsurpassed mathematical abilities.

Raymond could count many hundreds of toothpicks to the exact number as soon as they fell to the floor. He mentally computed with accuracy difficult multiplication questions, before others could even begin to push buttons on calculators.

Yet at an airport with his brother, a fast-paced entrepreneur played by Tom Cruise, Raymond's ability to calculate went haywire. Fear of a potential jet crash made this mathematical genius panic.

Raymond screamed every time a potential airline was mentioned for him to fly on. As soon as each available air carrier was mentioned, Raymond hollered the date one of its planes had crashed, the place, and the number of people killed.

When Raymond finally mentioned that Quantas was the only major airline that never had a fatal crash, his angry brother realized that the Australian carrier didn't serve the American airport. Raymond's "illogical" tirades forced the brothers to take their cross-country trip to Los Angeles by car. Audiences roared.

Life Itself Is A Roulette Wheel

Euclid, an Egyptian teacher 300 years before Christ and known as the "father of logic," might have gotten a healthy chuckle out of Raymond's tirades.

From the same era, the great philosopher Aristotle became convinced it's natural for people to study every aspect of nature, and that "blind chance" fails to rule the universe.

Undoubtedly motivated by either fear or a conclusion that he would be executed, Aristotle fled Macedonia after his former student, King Alexander the Great, died in 323 B.C.

Martin Luther, whose defiance inaugurated the Protestant Reformation, faced possible burning at the stake for his protest against the Catholic Church in 1521. Luther's anger had pushed him past the point of possible fear, when he nailed his now-famous Ninety-Five Theses to a Hamburg church door.

For Americans horrified by the thought of terrorists, it might be interesting to know that Pope Urban II sparked a war against Muslims. On Nov. 27, 1095, Urban II gave a rousing speech to mere thousands of people in France.

His charismatic tone and fervor caused so much passion and anger that Christians launched the first of the Crusades to recapture the Holy Land, a massive military campaign that filled many of its victims with terror.

A different brand of fear struck Christopher Columbus' three-ship fleet after it set sail from Span on Aug. 3, 1492. Horrified of the unknown some frightened sailors under Columbus' command wished to turn back.

As most schoolchildren know, the undaunted Columbus insisted on continuing to head west despite some fears that they might "fall of the edge of the Earth."

While fear remains constant as a condition of being human, each American generation has had to face a different brand of terror.

George Washington's troops struggled through fears they would starve or freeze to death during the American Revolution.

At Gettysburg during the American Civil War, President Abraham Lincoln saw firsthand that the apparent lack of fear—or at least pushing such thoughts aside—could lead to thousands of deaths in a single day.

During World War II in France, American soldiers were under orders to show nothing but "bravery" as they jumped from foxholes, ran toward the enemy and got shot down by the thousands. From the other side, the German enemy suffered similar casualties.

This Isn't the First "Terror" War in the USA

Prior to September 2001, at least two terrorist wars had already been fought on American soil. The battle against Native Americans in the 1600s, 1700s, 1800s, and well into the 1900s marked a four-centuries campaign.

"Big Brother," the white man and his government, terrorized and eradicated millions. Entire races or tribes were wiped into extinction. American settlers became "terrorists." And although many Indians responded with their own terrorism-style tactics, their adversaries prevailed.

In the early part of the 20th Century, especially in the 1920s, it became the U.S. government fighting terrorists on American soil. These warriors were labeled "mobsters," the likes of Al Capone, Baby Faced Nelson and John Dillinger. Mobsters weren't called terrorists at the time, but they certainly behaved that way in every sense of the word.

Like Middle Eastern and Southern Asia countries—and even greedy corporations—that cause worry today, the U.S. government's anti-Indian cavalries and the Chicago Mob were bullies who would have been useless to negotiate with.

Cavalries and mobsters browbeat, whipped, shot and killed their victims, often striking with little or no warning. Each terrorist group ignited fear in its enemy, as sudden death and destruction spread nationwide.

CHAPTER EIGHT

Bravery or Cowardice?

U.S. history and world history leave just as many unanswered questions as they do answers about fear. What's clear is that fear and ways to handle it are just as deep-rooted in the American culture as the colors red, white and blue.

Some folks might say that without fear, we could not have bravery, for it's only by getting past terror that people achieve freedom.

From the moment American astronaut Neil Armstrong became the first man to step on the moon on July 20, 1969, Americans knew they had overcome some potential fears.

We stepped past fear when President Harry Truman made the difficult and still-controversial decision to kill tens of thousands of Japanese with nuclear bombs in August 1945 in Hiroshima and Nagasaki. And fear of being psychologically captive for generations subsided Jan. 20, 1981; that's the day Ronald Reagan was inaugurated as president for the first time, and 52 American hostages were released after 444 days in captivity in Iran.

In a sense, Americans have always been locked in fear or at least faced with it, no matter what challenges they had to overcome. There's always another obstacle, another road not traveled, another villain who wants destruction, and another natural disaster that kills hundreds or thousands of people.

Fear will remain an integral part of American culture long after the last vein of these current terrorists is squeezed into obliteration—both on the war battle front and in the arena of corporate terrorism spawned by lobbyists.

Fear is not only integral to our very survival, it plays a major role in motivating us to achieve, whether we eventually fail or succeed. Emblazoned with this knowledge, let's realize *fear can be a good thing*.

As Americans we know how to overcome fear's potential roadblocks. We can and should allow our hearts to open up to the many positive possibilities, doorways to success that only fear can allow us to perceive. Any prayers for those who have died, and good wishes to a bright future, are heard by the courageous.

For generations to come, Americans should realize fear is nothing but a dusty old doormat. Each of us can clean our feet off on its worn-out surface, before entering our living rooms, workplaces and entertainment venues. Thanks to our ancestors' sacrifices and our own struggles, we deserve nothing less than clean shoes.

News Flash! More Destructive Weapons!

Consider technology a curse or a blessing. What's commonly referred to as "man's inhumanity to man" easily could be labeled "People's ingenuity against people."

From the days when early humans first ventured from their trees and caves, people have constantly been upgrading, improving and refining their weapons. Fists got replaced by rocks, which were replaced by crude hatchets, which were replaced by spears, and so on.

Killing devices of the 17th Century were replaced by "better" technologies in the 18th Century, and a never-ending process that continues today.

Military personnel can thank Alfred Nobel for stepping up death and destruction a great notch in 1866 when he invented dynamite. In what some people consider one of history's greatest ironies, the same inventor launched the annual Nobel Peace Prize. That coveted award honors those who do their utmost to prevent war while advancing peace.

Each new invention of destruction brings more fear and death. In 1862, Richard Gatling of North Carolina created the first machine gun, the Gatling Gun. An eventual 10-barrel version capable of whipping off 360 rounds per minute became as feared as moats and swords had been in the Middle Ages.

The U.S. Army purchased three Gatling Guns in 1865. Not to be outdone, nations throughout Europe bought similar devices.

Like the best and most notorious weapons of each previous generation, dynamite and the Gatling Gun struck fear in the souls of people who learned of them.

Worries spread fast that such weapons could destroy humanity or at least civilizations. Many believed these contraptions could obliterate entire countries if given a chance.

Never satisfied at the amount of fear and death each new weapon brings, military brass continually strived to improve them. Eager to increase death on the battlefield, in 1902 "clever" U.S. generals and their trusted underlings hooked electric motors to Gatling Guns to increase firepower.

Yet high production costs and the lack of any current battles forced the Army to discontinue production of its improved Gatling. Then, World War I brought a sudden rush of weaponry unseen in any previous conflict.

Tanks, gun-laden aircraft and mustard gas changed the landscape of killing.

Each era seemed to forget previous generations. Every new war's soldiers and its citizen-victims believed they were the first that ever had to face new fears of mass destruction.

Of the many technological "marvels" of the 20th Century, the rush to improve killing machines kept well ahead of the pack. World War II brought aircraft carriers, paratroopers, buzz bombs, and the dreaded kamikaze pilot—each suicide-bound flyer accepting a mission to give his life for the Japanese Empire.

Unexpected, sudden suicide bombings intensified fear and terror in the Vietnam War in the 1960s and 1970s. U.S. fighter jets, fast-moving helicopters and napalm rushed onto the military scene.

Yet these updated devices failed to enable the United States to conquer its enemy, which relied on time-tested guerrilla warfare to thwart defenses and crush morale.

Embraced by the Chinese thousands of years ago, time-tested tactics of bravery, the art of surprise and cunning remained essential. Age-old tactics proved that even "new-improved" weaponry isn't necessarily mightier than the mind of man and his willingness to persevere.

The Battles Will Continue Amid Increasing Fear

Without question the current War on Terrorism—and the global economic crisis, for that matter—is like a baby volcano, erupting mounds of "new" killing devices. And yet, like that famous saying claims, "Everything old is new again." Our minds have convinced us that since we're the first to face this brand of destruction, then surely we must be the last.

We all trembled in the wake of the Attack on America. We told ourselves that "no generation has ever had to go through this. How will we survive?"

Well, amid our current struggles, such worries would come as little solace to many. Fear and the lack of historical perspective, coupled with a solemn sense of the current moment, leave us confused and bewildered.

Amid rampant deregulation approved by Congress, the greediest American corporate executives joined the ranks of the worst, most vicious terrorists without us even knowing it—through the 1990s and well into this century.

With many thousands of lobbyists as their foot soldiers, some greedy corporate leaders waged war on America—convincing Congress to remove or relax vital regulations on business. This, in turn, contributed greatly to the massive global economic downturn.

Besides unfathomable amounts of cash for lobbyists, corporate executives used silent weapons to carry out their orders—systems that didn't exist a hundred years earlier, everything from emails to online meeting systems.

To these corporate terrorists, the American worker became the enemy, and so countless millions of those jobs were eliminated—severely crippling the backbone of our economy.

While all this was underway, till the severe economic downturn that began in September 2008, most from the American middle-class had been unaware of what the "corporate fat cats" were doing to them.

If these victims had known at the time what was being planned for them, would they have been afraid? Would investors through the first seven years of this Century have been gripped with worry, if they know what the greedy corporate executives had in store for their portfolios?

Another Challenge Always Emerges

We allow it-has-never-happened-before sensations to wallop us in the gut. Just about every time we open a newspaper, hear a radio or turn on TV a similar message rushes to the brain.

Anthrax attacks spread, terrorists fly jets into buildings, high-paid corporate lobbyists plot selfish schemes at the hands of politicians, and the "evil ones" have the audacity to kill countless thousands of innocent people.

Our minds and senses tell us these atrocities have ***never happened before***.

And yet for the most part, all this has happened before and it will happen again in the future—if history is an indication! Only weapons and characters change.

As long as there is an "enemy" capable of using weapons in its possession, that adversary will attack if given a chance and when motivated by a charismatic despot.

We all were born into a world where this true-life scenario happens again and again without letup. You and all your relatives were born into a world where ***war happens***.

The cycle of war and apparent peace remains as constant as birth and death from subsequent generations.

Once again, the Roulette Wheel of Fate comes to play. Fears that might seem "illogical" in one instance become "logical" in another. Fear of getting on a plane might seem silly considering the "odds." Such mental terror pales against the notion of war.

Putting this into clear perspective, chances of being in a commercial jet crash are astronomical, partly because "only" a few hundred people—or even a "few thousand" people—are usually victims.

Yet when war erupts and severe global economic crisis spreads, chances are far greater that you or someone you know will be affected, *because a single war or global economic Depression impacts far more people throughout a far greater geographic area than does a single plane crash.*

Anyone who wants to learn to manage fear must accept such horrors as an unchangeable "reality." Acceptance occurs in much the way one is forced to face his inevitable death.

Indeed, historians remain hard-pressed to find a single year since the beginning of recorded history when there wasn't at least one war on Earth. If life is truly a mix between continual good and evil, of peace and war, then you truly were born into a predictable mix.

The ebb and flow of waves tickling sandy shores are as constant as your heartbeat, and as reliable as the unwritten guarantee that war or severe economic hardship will erupt in your lifetime.

People who are agnostic and those filled with religious faith all were born to face fear, often at the hands of national conflict or international disputes. To deny that reality is to deny you are alive.

Whether by "fate" if that's your belief, or simply plane old "bad luck," there is no getting around the fact we're at war on battle fronts and in the financial realm. It bears repeating, then, that there is a possibility you will die during this conflict or that your children and grandchildren will be killed by terrorists, or become homeless.

During your lifetime, these scenarios either will happen or they won't.

That said, when "destruction in your immediate environment" came, if it did, you would have to make many decisions. Whether to run or fight, and whether to be "brave" or "scared," are among options you would have to consider.

Even today, born into this dastardly situation, your only physical escape will be your own death or "national victory." Yet even after such a win, threats of other attacks or wars still loom.

A Question of How to Exist

For Shakespeare's "Hamlet," a primary question prevailed after his father's death by murder. "To be, or not to be, that is the question," the mournful young Hamlet mourned.

This character's inner inspection beams within us all. Like that son of a king, we each must decide if and how to persevere.

And while realizing there's no escaping the sands of time and the realities of our world, we can consider these wars on economic crisis and on terrorism as opportunities to achieve.

There's a legacy awaiting our children, either their own deaths during youth or perhaps a chance to live to a ripe old age. In what Charles Darwin hailed in his timeless classic "Origin of the Species," we're faced with "the struggle for existence" and the "survival of the fittest."

No timid fighter ever won an Olympic gold in boxing, just as no under-armed nation ever survived short-term ravages of an all-out attack by a vastly superior foe.

No matter what weapons are developed, no matter what "new" creative battle styles are used, the victor almost universally happens to be the one who shows the most courage, perseverance, preparation and willpower.

If you decide to give up hope and let new weaponry—everything from bombs to cutting-edge new banking systems to email—to intimidate you, odds are great that you'll fail to realize your quest for happiness. Embrace the notion of getting past fright, and find a potion for getting inner strength.

Take the option from Hamlet's query, that decision to "be" and to *evolve into what you need to be to survive and prosper*.

Learn to understand and grasp what you already know deep down, the blessing of inspiration. In this light, you're able to shine as a star, lifting the arms of your inner spirit and praising life.

So, take this journey.

And accept the existence of unchangeable realities, the Five Ws: "Wickedness, Weaponry, War, Weeping and Weariness."

Then, realize it's okay to be scared and to worry about potential outcomes. All along, it's also acceptable to get past fear, and to allow yourself to enter a mental space where self-fulfilling sensations prevail.

The "Brave" Can Become "Weak"

World-famous author Margaret Mitchell arguably described the intricacies of fear and all other war-related emotions far better than any other writer. Yet in real-life, her failure to have an appropriate level of fear caused her to lose her life.

At age 49, in 1949 Mitchell failed to use the learned-fear reaction of looking both ways when attempting to walk across a street. Lacking enough "sensible fear," she also didn't use a crosswalk. On Peachtree Street, an Atlanta boulevard mentioned in Mitchell's epic, classic Civil War novel "Gone With the Wind," a taxi driven by drunken cabbie Hugh Gravitt mowed her down.

Mitchell failed to take "sensible" action, to use fear—or at least worry—when it's appropriate. Unless we have a death wish, none of us should consider ourselves invincible. A mere image of being invincible also fails to protect people from fears that life forces us to confront.

TV's first Superman, actor George Reeve, died of a gunshot in an apparent suicide, reported depressed by his inability to find other significant film roles—deep seeded fears that he would never succeed on film without a superhero's cape. Ironically, just a few decades earlier, Reeve had a bit part in the film "Gone With the Wind."

Decades later, the late 20th Century movie Superman, Christopher Reeves, became paralyzed after a horse-riding accident. Would a better "learned-fear" reaction have saved this beloved star from suffering a life-changing injury—which eventually led to his death at age 52, nine years after the accident?

Blessed with more courage than fright, Reeves was quoted as saying he considered killing himself after the accident—but then decided to launch his career as a film director.

People whose heroics help us win wars sometimes suffer fear, shock or other mental traumas that damage their psyches.

World War II Medal of Honor winner Audie Murphy blamed post-traumatic stress syndrome or "battle fatigue" on severe tensions during his last years. Contrary to urban legend, Murphy didn't commit suicide but was killed while a passenger in a plane crash.

Of course, the accident ended Murphy's mental horrors. And according to an official report, his grave is the second most visited at Arlington National Cemetery, behind the writer of "Profiles in Courage," President John F. Kennedy.

Virgil "Gus" Grissom, considered by many as among the USA's bravest astronauts, survived after his Liberty Bell 7 Mercury capsule sank to the bottom of the Atlantic in 1961.

Contrary to the beliefs of many people, some folks insisted that Grissom panicked after his otherwise routine splashdown—blowing an emergency exit hatch, thereby causing the capsule to sink.

Nearly six years later, Grissom proved he still had plenty of gumption. He died a hero on Jan. 27, 1967, along with two other Apollo astronauts when fire raced through their capsule on a launch pad.

Meriwether Lewis, part of the famous Lewis & Clark exploration team, braved the unknown in helping lead America's first official westbound expedition through the USA wilderness to the Pacific Ocean.

After Lewis returned east as a national hero, President Thomas Jefferson appointed him governor of Louisiana. Those duties proved more stressful to Lewis than conquering the great outdoors. Less than a decade after the cross-country expedition, Lewis died of an apparent suicide in Tennessee.

Lewis' personal tragedy exemplifies mankind's imperfections, its complexity and its unpredictability. To proclaim that the chance of war is certain during any single generation is not to say that each outcome or its degree of fear can be predicted with accuracy.

Indeed, during times of war and national peace, fear is a cruel joker, a wicked wildcard that seems to play the game of life however it wants.

How to Eliminate Fear

America: "Home of the Brave"

While many of their comrades persevere and manage to "get on" with their lives, the bravest soldiers have been known to crumble into babbling masses of flesh after incalculable amounts of stress jolts their spirits.

Burly John Wayne types sometimes crack mentally, lose all appetite, and enter insane asylums. Shock, worry and fright often prevail, causing more damage than mere bullets and bombs.

The notion that war and economic stress is "natural" gets blown to smithereens. Just because great battles and financial strife have happened constantly since civilization began doesn't mean it's easy or acceptable to the human psyche.

Yes, war is both "the most natural human condition" and "the most unnatural thing of all." Here's a paradox that sizzles like a red-hot poker, a realization that's especially dangerous as the Attack on America and the Great Depression II expand into other nations and societies—not to mention our own.

It has been said that anyone who has been in a war loses, whether his country wins or not. No person should have to witness and undergo heated battle or severe economic hardship or homelessness caused by corporate greed.

Fear, joy, love, ecstasy and hate all mean nothing when a bomb blasts 25 feet away from you—followed right away by another explosion and another, and another in seemingly countless repetition.

The result often becomes shell shock. War veterans proclaim that some people seem to lose fear under such conditions, doing what they "need" to do, while others become petrified and incapable of action. Individual reactions depend on people involved.

Take away food, water, and shelter during prolonged battle and animal-like reactions surface. To survive, warriors sometimes fight as if filled with the fervor of a Bengal tiger gnawing madly upon its prey. Other combatants succumb, their spirits overcome.

If a terrorist's bomb blows in the middle of your city, town or community, there's no question you'll be afraid or mentally numbed. Yet that's not to say you'll react with fear, different from being "merely afraid."

As you consider your values, it might be helpful to remember these other instances where fear causes confusion—even among the most brave:

Sergeant York: At an Army camp training soldiers for World War I, officers had to convince Sgt. Alvin C. York to undergo target practice. The future hero seemed fearful at the prospect of killing anyone, or even shooting at the shadow image of a human being. "Sir, I am doing wrong. Practicing to kill people is against my religion," York told his superiors. After managing to overcome his "fears" or concerns about killing others, York won the Medal of Honor for killing 25 Germans, capturing 132 prisoners and knocking out 35 machine guns at the Battle of the Argonne Forest in the fall of 1918.

General Patton: Was it a deep-seeded fear of being afraid that motivated legendary World War II Gen. George Patton to slap one of his soldiers, a man who had been hospitalized after suffering shell shock? After Gen. Dwight Eisenhower forced Patton to apologize to his troops for the slapping incident, Patton moved on to lead his armies and the allies to victory. Ironically, it may have been Patton's apparent failure to have enough "learned-fear" reaction for him to avoid an accident—which resulted in his own fatal injuries.

Carole Lombard: This gorgeous movie star, beloved wife of famed actor Clark Gable, is an example of conquering fear and dying for mankind. Lombard was among 22 TWA Skysleeper passengers killed when it crashed in Nevada as they were returning to the West Coast from a U.S. War Bond fund-raising rally in Indiana. The crash occurred less than a half-hour after the Los Angeles-bound plane took off from Las Vegas.

Roberto Clemente: It may have been fear of poverty and enough courage to help people escape its ravages that led this legendary baseball star's death. Clemente died in 1972 in a plane crash at age 38, while flying relief supplies to Nicaraguan earthquake victims.

Freddie Prinze Sr.: Was it a lack of enough fear, or maybe even a feeling of invulnerability that led to the apparent suicide of popular Latino comedian Freddie Prinze? Star of the popular 1970s sitcom "Chico and the Man," Prinze died at age 22 of suicide from a gunshot wound as his fame skyrocketed.

Some of these instances mark cases where people either had too much fear, not enough of it or were unable to recognize how it could be used. Because we're human, we don't always manage our fears the right way, ignore its warnings or simply fail to realize that *there are times we should be afraid, because doing so will enable us to survive*.

Listen to Your Heart

Rock star Ritchie Valens reportedly had premonitions he would die in a plane crash, but he took a flight anyway on the last night of his life. He made this decision in order to avoid having to take a bus.

On the date now widely proclaimed as the "day the music died," Feb. 3, 1959, Valens could have accepted an offer for ground transportation. He and other famous victims, Buddy Holly and J.P. "The Big Bopper" Richardson, *didn't know they were supposed to be afraid*.

Quite a number of other famous musicians died in plane crashes. Country crooner John Denver of "Rocky Mountain High" fame couldn't deal with his fears and addictions to alcohol, but he was brave enough to fly. Apparently lacking adequate learned-fear behaviors, at age 53 Denver may have failed to check for appropriate fuel levels in his small aircraft before it plummeted into California's Monterey Bay in October 1997.

And was it fear of being near her husband, portrayed in the media as being abusive, that motivated country great Patsy Cline to take her fateful, final private plane trip in 1963?

Yes, sometimes, during both national peacetime and war, having fear or not doesn't matter—or it can mean everything in increasing chances of survival.

So, take comfort in realizing there are things you'll never "know," sometimes until it's too late. Often we live or die by our choices. From deciding whether to smoke or to exercise, or a wide range of other activities, our behaviors mean everything or sometimes they mean nothing at all.

As far as this situation with terrorists and with greedy corporate executives, their lobbyists and politicians, everything you do may not make a difference in guaranteeing your survival, or it could mean saving your life.

You could build a 100-foot-deep bomb shelter for yourself and your family, only to discover too late that terrorists have shoved a 5,000-pound bomb down its entrance.

Or, you could go through the hassle and expense of constructing a sanctuary, only to find our government has slaughtered all terrorists and that your building project had been unnecessary. Remember, as we've already made clear, you're the master of things you can control, in ways you can and want.

Ultimately, all this comes down to the acknowledgement that whatever happens is going to occur. All you can do is your best or your worst, or even be mediocre, whatever you want along the way. So, take comfort in reviewing words such as those in the copyrighted 1956 Doris Day hit song, "Que Sera, Sera."

"Now, I have children of my own. They ask their mother, 'What will I be? Will I be handsome? Will I be rich? I tell them tenderly … Que Sera, Sera. Whatever will be, will be; the future's not ours to see. Que sera, sera. What will be, will be."

CHAPTER NINE

Sudden Attack & Then React

These days you might wonder how you would react, if a group of terrorists barged through your front door and into your living room. Under such a situation, if they carried hand grenades and pointed rifles at your family, you probably would have some kind of reaction.

Oddly, perhaps you'd show indifference, and try to watch TV as long as possible. However unlikely that might seem, people have been known to stay glued to the boob tube during crisis.

Fearful of facing the truth, rather than tell authorities or call funeral homes, some grieving relatives have allowed their dead spouses' bodies to stay at home for months or even for years.

A world-famous, Pulitzer Prize-winning Vietnam War photo of a naked girl running down a road, crying in fear as she escaped a bomb blast remains locked in the psyche. Evard Munch's eternal 1893 painting "The Scream," the epitome of internal fear, terror and fright, still draws so much reaction that many companies have used forms of it for advertisements.

Attempting to use fear to motivate voters in the 1964 presidential campaign proved so controversial that a TV ad aired only once. The Lyndon Johnson campaign ad featured a little girl at ground zero moments before a nuclear attack, as an announcer counted down.

Some analysts concluded the advertisement convinced Americans that GOP presidential candidate Sen. Barry Goldwater would have used the bomb. Johnson won.

Previous Education Motivated By Fear

Maybe it was some sort of misguided need to feel in control that motivated officials to give school children foolhardy instruction in the 1950s. Youngsters often were rehearsed in the art of putting their bodies under their school desks, practicing for the possibility of a nuclear attack.

Some children were led to believe such actions might save them during a nuclear war, when in fact a direct hit would have caused instant obliteration. Could this educational program have been a way to make people feel more in control, eliminating fears?

People coast-to-coast insisted on building bomb shelters at their own homes during that decade. From the 1960s through the 1980s, the threat of a nuclear attack on the United States remained just as real.

Yet through that period, construction of such shelters subsided. Odds of an attack remained just as great. Society had managed to put itself into a state of continual denial.

Faced with their imminent deaths during battle and during peaceful situations, people either knowingly or unwittingly allow their souls to spring forth. Those who are doomed often utter quirky statements, the strangest things imaginable in their final moments.

Faced with certain doom, many dying people brush aside any notion of fear. According to some historians, as Marie Anotinette, Queen of France, was marched to the guillotine in 1793, this royal beauty stepped on her executioner's foot. "Monsieur, I beg your pardon," she proclaimed, not long before the blade sliced off her head.

In his final statement before being executed in 1995, killer Thomas J. Grasso proclaimed, "I did not get my Spaghetti-Os; I got spaghetti. I want the press to know this."

Fear Makes Us Unpredictable

Such oddball statements by doomed people show that individuals who have at least a little time to prepare for death often are able to hide or deny their apparent horrors. Destruction always tastes sour, but such people sometimes make it sweet.

"Either the wallpaper goes, or I do," writer Oscar Wilde said during his final moments in 1900. Showing just as much courage as his reputation dictated, President George Washington told those present, "I die hard, but I'm not afraid to go."

To be sure, the terror of the unknown can and is overcome by values, personal beliefs of a brighter future—the belief of a "nirvana," either here on Earth or in an afterlife.

As if to promise that she was ready to be an angel, just before her final breath in 1931, ballerina Anna Pavlova said, "Get my swan costume ready."

Others are motivated by nothing but hate for anyone and everyone on the planet, thinking nothing but the worst during those final moments as the Grim Reaper approaches.

In 1970, TV newscaster Chris Hubbock shot herself live on the air— but only after saying: "And now, in keeping with Channel 40's policy of always giving you blood and guts, in living color, you're about to see another first, an attempted suicide." Hubbock died 14 hours later.

Deciding whether it's "insane" to lose fear comes down to a matter of perspective. One person's idea of kooky is another's vision of reasonable, sometimes after heated battle. The final words of American Revolution War General Ethan Allen were enough to chill the spine. For many of us who value freedom Allen's bold statement remains a cause for inspiration.

"Waiting are they? Waiting are they?" Allen wailed, courageous to the end, while responding to an attending doctor who said he feared angels were awaiting the general's soul. "Well, let 'em wait."

To be sure, many good Americans have remained defiant, bull-headed in refusing to budge in the name of what they think is "right."

If you decide to get feisty and face fears against terrorism and against economic hardship, you don't need to be brave, or a fool, or even level-headed. Indeed, it's not always "just ourselves" we think about when facing possible destruction.

To be a self-fulfilled part of the human race means caring for other people at the worst of times. Some people might argue that to be fearful of terrorists or greedy corporations is to be self-centered, worried only about values of doom and gloom rather than focusing on the needs and desires of loved ones.

Graced with love for humanity, actress Ethyl Barrymore gasped deep-felt concerns moments before her death: "Is everybody happy? I want everybody to be happy. I know I'm happy."

True to the spirit of the USA, Barrymore's final words marked the very essence of what many of us believe it is to be an American. Those words "life, liberty and the pursuit of happiness" are in the Declaration of Independence, strong and succinct depictions of our purpose. To ignore them is to deny the core of our nation.

The need to feel worthwhile, as if we've contributed somehow to this mass of confusing worldwide behavior remains powerful. No matter where a person hails from, there's almost always a need to be thought of as courageous, as fearless, and being focused.

"Don't let it end like this," Mexican revolutionary Pancho Villa said as he died in 1923. "Tell them I said something."

Acknowledge Present Realities

No matter what is said or unsaid, no matter how a person behaves right before the moment of his death, an undeniable truth remains. Before death can occur, there must be life.

If you want to be among the living, to enjoy a fulfilling journey toward your own inevitable demise, you will have to acknowledge present events.

Amid this war on terrorism and economic struggle, there are flowers being sold in shops, parents are crying out with joy at the births of their first children, and some kids are hopping up and down in delight—overjoyed by their first visit from the Tooth Fairy.

Sure, tears run deep at sudden deaths from tragedies and from natural causes. Horrible things happen daily as The Human Project proceeds on its journey. Throughout it all, too much of any one thing can be considered "evil."

From some people's view, eating too much food can be considered evil because doing so can make you fat. Too much gambling can be considered evil, because it can break your personal bank account. And too much exercise, far in excess of what might be considered reasonable, might get labeled as evil because it takes you away from your family and other potential "bad habits."

By contrast, any of these activities in moderation might be considered sensible. Eating proper amounts of nutritious foods, gambling just enough to have fun, and exercising to the degree necessary to keep in shape might be considered reasonable.

Taking all this a step further, at least from some people's view, it might be considered "evil" to worry too much about terrorism or about economic hardship.

The argument here might be that such excessive worries overwhelm a person, robbing him of other qualities he might enjoy. Imagine spending your life focused on such attacks.

On the flip side of this equation, ponder the possibilities of having merely moderate degrees of concern about such threats. If you believe moderation is preferable when it comes to concerns about terrorism, then it's a good idea to focus on your personal value system.

In this vein, consider your own values, if any, and what you label as "right" and "wrong." At least for yourself, define limits of proper or acceptable behaviors or reactions.

Then, after some reflection, you're on course for fear management.

Blessed Are the Fearful

"My dog's better than your dog! My dog's better than yours! My dog's better"—because he eats a certain type of food.

So went a 1960s TV commercial, geared to children and their parents. Hook, line and sinker, this pitch yanked at the gut of human emotion. The yearning to be better than other people, to have more might over them, and to "win" often prevails.

Fears of being the underdog, of having less, of not being "better" than a neighbor can motivate armies. Rather than merely being whipped or beaten by an adversary, real or perceived, what could be worse than not emerging victorious?

From many perspectives, the American way mandates continual struggles and advances, often for the primary and sole purpose of overpowering an opponent. Losing "sucks" from the American viewpoint.

Forget the fact it's cool and politically correct to say, "It's not how you win or lose, it's how you play the game."

Add to this the realization that when church matters get involved, complexities intensify because the USA is a diverse society. Many of us have vastly different beliefs and value systems than our neighbors.

One person's idea of a "sin" is another fellow's acceptable or even mandatory delight. From matters of pornography to educational preferences, our demands are as vast as our languages, religions, and complex demographic characteristics.

Fear of possible or actual religious persecution motivated many of our nation's original inhabitants to come to U.S. soil. Blessed with courage, others immigrated merely because they wanted a better way of living. Our melting pot filled with diverse faiths, spiced by agnostics who embrace no religion.

Deep within the bowels of this swelling nation, during our colonial period we already were striving for religious "tolerance." Our forefathers who signed the USA's Declaration of Independence, and later its constitution, made it clear the "separation of church and state" were essential to its new government.

A subsequent mass of immigrants was guaranteed they'd never have to face fear of persecution due to their religious beliefs.

By the time the last shot was fired in the American Revolution, our politicians were busy striving to ensure people would have rights to worship their own gods. A vast majority were Christians, as religious tolerance became a mandate. To persecute others for their beliefs was considered "un-American."

Amid the wars on terrorism and corporate greed, herein rests a challenge as some Americans persecute their fellow citizens who are of the Muslim faith. Some "innocent" U.S. residents of Middle Eastern or South Asian descent have been tormented. Afraid to be in public, a number of them have been shot, spit upon or beaten.

A Paradox, a Cruel Reality

Those who attacked Muslims or African Americans within our culture are a distinct minority of Americans. That doesn't soothe frazzled nerves of victims. Violence intensifies fears among Muslim Americans and people of color.

The fact their country is being targeted by warrior terrorists causes rightful concern among Americans in the Muslim faith. Domestic hate worsens the situation.

Ironically, since 2001, and especially since the economic downturn that intensified in September 2008, many people of numerous religions have been flocking to their churches in record numbers.

Suddenly, folks from all walks of life have found faith to ease their fears and to calm their worries. They're positive or at least hopeful that their god will alleviate fear, give them courage to persevere, and to end the wars on terrorism and financial crisis.

If these same worshippers stopped to think about it, though, they'd realize most wars are caused by religion! Some of the same churches the timid among us embrace for solace have sparked and encouraged long, seemingly endless wars.

So, should one be fearful of churches, at a time when faith seems more important than ever? Goodness knows, life seems complicated enough without having these additional worries.

Religious intolerance attacked many faiths long before the Roman Empire. Church-backed nations with the largest armies pummeled those of different beliefs. Victors ordered their conquered victims to adopt certain religions or suffer death.

Taking the "might makes right" concept to the extreme, conquerors carried out their threats and killed those who refused.

Considering all this today, where can a person turn? Is it OK to get involved in a church that has encouraged mass destruction, even if in a different place and time? Should local and international churches be forgiven because, after all, "what's in the past is in the past?"

Unless you're the type who accepts everything he's told, no one but yourself can answer these questions. In learning to manage your fears, you can and must set values. Paramount among these efforts is deciding who you are, what you want out of life, and your degree of commitment to any religious belief system.

In this sense, each of us is almost like Jordan, a key character in Ernest Hemingway's classic novel, "For Whom the Bell Tolls." At the end of this tale involving the Spanish Civil War, a shell wounds Jordan as he and his comrades try to escape on horseback.

But Jordan is unable to continue fleeing with them, so his comrades must consider the option of shooting him to save him from having to undergo a painful death.

Although he's brave enough to be shot, and he realizes that would end his torment, Jordan refuses to take such a remedy. Out of respect for life, he doesn't want his comrades to snub out another human being.

Instead, Jordan accepts from his fellow soldiers a machine gun, which he can use to defend himself when the enemy arrives.

Like Jordan, each of us has been "wounded" to varying degrees by the Attack on America and by The Great Depression II. For most, the suffering is mental rather than physical, still a potentially challenging situation.

If we want, we can take a variety of remedies in attempts to alleviate fears and pain. Alcohol, illegal drugs, over-medication, and plane old denial are among many short-term prescriptions.

Just as Jordan did, however, we can refuse any easy "fix" that might seem to alleviate our hurt. And like Jordan, we can make a difficult or controversial choice, whether it's adopting a newfound moral conviction or embracing an old reliable religion, taking solace in a church we've always known and loved.

As we float across this reflective pond, a proverbial Bell of Freedom tolls for all of us. It tolls within our hearts, echoing in the knowledge we can face such life-changing decisions.

Today, your heart tells you what you believe. If you put yourself in a quiet place, and if you can become calm, your soul will give you answers. And your mind will remain the biggest weapon.

The Hands of Time Stood Still

Television stations and radio broadcasters interrupted their programming on May 13, 1997. Much of the USA and many other sections of the world followed news reports in shock, disbelief and horror.

People followed every word as if their lives depended on the outcome. The news media rushed to the scene in a small town. Some journalists reacted as if this would be the greatest and most important tragedy of their lives.

So much of the news media focused on Midland, Texas, that many

Americans were soon talking about an unexpected tragedy there. Each word on the development brought bated breaths from everyday folks nationwide, and prayers of hope from church leaders everywhere. No, there hadn't been a horrible chemical accident killing hundreds of people. And no, the desperate situation had nothing to do with a military attack, or a natural disaster such as a hurricane.

The victim was just one person, 18-month-old Jessica McClure. A nationwide sensation ensued when the little girl fell 22 feet down a well. Trapped far down in the hole, which reportedly was as little as 8 inches wide in some places, little Jessica clung to life.

Fear for Jessica gripped hundreds of millions of people. Fear spread worldwide. Fear intensified, worry that just one person among billions of people on this planet would die.

The first day signaled an undisputable truth, that most of us within the human race care about each other—even those we've never met.

Worries increased to the maximum level because Jessica was a child, helpless and unable to do anything significant to save herself. In today's wars on terrorism and on economic hardship, the situation is much the same.

In many cases, our fears mark concerns for others, more than just for ourselves. While despicable behaviors such as battles, political assassinations and common murders get most publicity, except on rare occasions such as Jessica's plight, man's love for his fellow human beings seems to take a back seat in the news business.

Today, if you're afraid for your children, spouse, siblings, parents and friends at the hands of terrorist warriors and of corporate mindlessness, you're not alone. Public opinion polls indicated many people worry just as much about their relatives as they do about themselves.

In some ways, at least, little Jessica's plight was similar to what most Americans feel today. She was trapped, in danger of suffocating. She was in darkness, unable to see light. She remained isolated from other human beings for much of the time, unable to eat food.

Those of us gripped with fear amid today's difficulties need to "escape" as well. Like Jessica had, we've got people trying to save us—our government, criminal investigators, the military and charitable organizations.

Jessica's rescuers included her neighbors, evacuation crews, and firefighters. Attempts to rescue her posed danger. Any effort to pull her up too fast might have caused a cave-in, resulting in suffocation.

And digging in from the side of the well could have caused the tunnel to collapse. Once again, similarities abound, when comparing Jessica's situation while in the hole to our own current plight.

Although we're obviously not trapped in a well, many of us worry that our government isn't doing enough, or that it has been doing the wrong things—situations that eventually might result in our deaths or homelessness.

Thanks to ingenuity and persistence, Jessica's rescuers managed to pull her out alive, 2 ½ days after the ordeal began. By contrast, our plight could last many years or even decades.

Our Challenging Journey Continues

Jessica's journey toward survival allowed us to see goodness within ourselves. Even today, her ordeal remains an example of the frailty of human life.

The good news for Jessica is that she's still alive. Things have changed around her, of course, such as developments in her family. Our government leaders promise that like her, we'll be able to get through this struggle and eventually move on to other concerns. Until that happens, though, many of us have a lengthy list of potential terrorist-related fears to deal with or to manage. During the first several years of this century, well before the severe international economic downturn of 2008, we already worried about not making money, and of losing the comforts of life.

Worries spread into almost every aspect of our lifestyles: that we wouldn't have enough enjoyment; that we'd lose our beautiful self images; and that our professional workloads would become a burden—not to mention the possibility of losing our jobs.

Some of us, especially politicians, hoped to avoid undue criticisms. Worries abounded that traumas would force us to age too quickly, that we'd lose our efficiencies and conveniences, and that mere survival would evolve into a difficult chore.

As humans, many of us naturally crave love and companionship, blessings we feared would be gone forever if our relatives or friends died.

Worsening matters, some of us became concerned about losing all our possessions, or that we'd never feel entertained again. Among the worst potential outcomes, we fretted over the possible permanent loss of our personal safety.

The notion of losing good health, of being unable to protect our families, of losing our sense of "superiority" left some of us stunned.

It was as if the entire planet had been pulled from under our feet. We ponder the possible loss of personal freedoms, as investigators intensify background checks.

Stressed to the max more than we ever realized was possible, we began generating many dreary scenarios. Has the excitement gone out of life forever? Will this "trend" of inner woe and anxiety remain?

Worsening matters, how can we trust major corporations, lobbyists, politicians and major charities to use our donations for the intended purpose? Can anyone be believed anymore?

Odd though this seems, although much has changed, much remains the same. At least as long as our basic infrastructure still stands, things like food delivery and the ability to turn on the lights, life goes on in much the way it had before—at least among those of us who have maintained income sources and shelter.

We could have worried about all these same exact things before the attacks and the financial downturn. At any time in our adult lives, we could worry about the loss of our jobs, our money, our personal freedoms, and even the loss of companionship.

In a sense, the situation is similar to the 1930s, when people in Germany hauled wheelbarrows full of cash—all of it worthless. By then, public opinion and human behaviors dictated that pieces of paper once deemed to have great value weren't worth a hoot anymore.

Excessive fear, and the inability to manage it, could create major problems. Here is among the best of many places possible to use that timeless quote made famous by President Franklin Delano Roosevelt, "We have nothing to fear but fear itself."

Without question, needless fear can bring down the homeland of America, for it's true that "a house divided cannot stand." Today, you have a chance to conquer negative thoughts. You can refuse to submit to the twin enemies of worry and woe.

Sure, the Twin Towers fell, thousands of Americans have died in Iraq, and our economy took a deep nosedive seven years after the attack. Yet within your spirit remains two other major towers, just as mighty in ways that really count.

First, you've got your mind; if you can control your mind well, you possess one of the most powerful forces in the universe. And second, you've got something *they* might try to take away, but which you can try to keep. Willpower, determination and stick-to-itiveness are all rolled up into one. Put those together with your mind as a traffic control tower and you can overcome adversity.

Yes, the "secret" is within your mind.

Now, will you learn how to use it?

CHAPTER TEN

3REST™ ~ *"Let's Roll!"*

At age 32, Todd Beamer was about to die at the hands of terrorists.

As an innocent passenger on a hijacked aircraft, Todd realized he and his fellow riders were doomed. Via cell phone, Todd's horrified wife told him that three other hijacked commercial airliners had crashed into buildings that morning.

Stunned, Todd and his fellow American passengers discussed what action to take. They made a difficult decision to fight.

"Let's roll."

Those were the last words Todd's wife heard him utter, a definite signal he and other passengers were about to storm the cockpit. The aircraft soon slammed into a Pennsylvania field, killing everyone on board.

In some ways, you're like Todd. Like he had to, you're about to make a decision to deal with fear. Todd's situation was probably different from yours likely is at this moment, because he was about to die.

There's at least one similarity. Like him, you're threatened by terrorism—either economic or via violence. And like him, you've got a choice to make.

Like him, you have a mind capable of making difficult decisions. By reading this, you're showing an effort to grasp and conquer a difficult situation.

So, let's conquer fear. **Let's roll.**

Setting yourself up for courage

Okay, now that we've identified the enemies—fear and its creators—it's time to cover quick definitions. Here, we prepare to list step-by-step solutions, now that we've made clear it's essential to prevent all forms of terrorism and economic hardships from wounding our psyches and spirits.

With patience and persistence, you'll be able to give some of this advice to others—either verbally or through your own actions. We hope results leave you happier, with a greater sense of freedom.

This section surely will make terrorists and greedy corporate executives angry. That's because you'll learn to identify your fears and to overcome them within as little as three days. You'll find an easy-to-follow action plan, before deciding how to react to certain situations. Then, review detailed tips, pointers on potential reactions.

Lessons here likely will help you in those areas of your life. Certain sections that at first might not seem like the most important areas emerge as vital to correcting your particular situation.

Before beginning, here is a quick review of what the initial basic sections will entail:

- **Identify fears:** You'll learn to identify your own fears. Whether you're in denial or not, it's essential that you seek out and destroy symptoms. 3REST™ is designed to help put you on track, enabling you to target "challenge" areas you may not have realized that you had.

- **Adopt an attitude:** 3REST™ seeks to enable you to analyze your war-related and economic-related fears and their impact on your lifestyle. Odds are great you'll "stumble" into a mirror of sorts, a reflection that reveals you have positive qualities you might not have realized.

- **Aim at your own heart**: Once nasty symptoms are identified, discover a gateway to your soul, blessed with eternal wisdom capable of fixing fear-caused challenges. Learn that the soul is "wise" beyond our comprehension. Within each of us rests a quiet and solemn area. Like all humans, you possess the heart and soul of a Muhammad, a Jesus Christ, a Buddha, and of a Gandhi.

Primary Benefits

Profit Spiritually: By eliminating symptoms, you'll be able to retain an essential energy. Find yourself renewed and refreshed, capable of charging through each day with re-found vitality. Allow your vigorous spirit to get free.

Profit Mentally: If perhaps you've found yourself in a state of "doldrums" since the Attack on America and since the severe international economic downturn, there's a chance in this freeing process that you'll discover yourself more mentally aware. This means getting blessed with an eternal wisdom, knowledge that it's okay to fear—as long as each reaction doesn't lock your behaviors beyond the limits of your personal values. You'll clearly realize the difference between a "knowing fear" and one that's realistic or self-limiting.

Benefit financially: By eliminating unwarranted fears, whether you have a job or not—or even if you're poor or wealthy—you'll realize what's important in your own life. And remember, when we speak about financially, we're talking about everything that involves worldly objects from money to furniture, your house and car and so on.

Fear's Failure Formula

Before discovering how to pass this "course," it's a good idea to know how to fail:

- Refuse to face fears.

- Refuse to admit there's a "problem."

- Lock yourself inside your home and never get out.

- Believe mindless BS that terrorist leaders and corporate executives sprout.

- Worry endlessly about every little scenario.

- Allow yourself to be "rigid" and unchangeable in this crisis.

- Refuse to generate creative solutions that'll help your lifelong learning and growth process continue.

- Refuse to learn these "secrets" and to do nothing but watch old "Andy Griffith" shows.

Framework to Begin

Briefly here as we begin the three-day process, remember it's essential to keep in mind basic elements of fear.

- **Fear motivates:** From cars we choose to clothes we buy and foods we eat, fear often is a driving factor. Pushing the so-called Fear Train into the opposite direction from its usual course, we see great promise for those who use this powerful engine wisely.

- **Contrary dream:** Some people benefit from fears that leave others feeling helpless. For instance, when stock prices plunge on certain days many people sell such investments as fast as possible. They fear loss. Yet this is when some buyers snatch up such securities. Are these buyers foolish? Not necessarily. From their perspective, prices have always rebounded over time. They might be wrong, but life itself is risk.

- **Good and bad fears:** "Bad" fears cause us to lose perspective and an ability to function well. "Good" fears happen when our hunches are right, protecting us. Herein rests a need for balance.

- **The need for fear:** Throughout our individual journeys through life, degrees of fears vary. Any "need" for individual fear depends on each person's perspective, moral values and motivations. Keep these factors in mind when evaluating yourself.

- **Choices:** In reviewing your own needs, values and risk limits, you have the ability to decide what's best for you. In much the same way, all of society on a local, regional, national and international basis must choose what it wants.

- **Lifelong learning:** Some answers won't be "simple" amid the continual Attack on America and the battle to bring justice to corporations and governments. Issues from anthrax to airlines and the meltdowns of financial institutions pose diverse challenges, solutions and reactions. What's best for one person is worst for the next. Only by making choices can we progress.

CHAPTER ELEVEN

3REST™ ~ Day 1 !

First, take heart in realizing that for many of us these lessons won't be difficult. It has been said that even a coward can conquer fear. President Thomas Jefferson hammered this home when he said, "The art of life is the art of avoiding pain, and he is the best pilot who steers clearest of the rocks and shoals, with which it is beset."

In order to conquer your own inner demons, you must recognize them. All the while, realize that even in noticing your concerns you may fail or even die, but at least you will have made a choice. On this first day, you'll become creative in tracking down your fears. You're a big-game hunter, after an enemy hidden in a forest.

Washington, D.C., postal worker Thomas Morris Jr.., called a 911 emergency line hours before he died of anthrax on Oct. 21, 2001. Morris realized he suffered symptoms that might have been caused by spores. Caution and worry weren't enough to save Morris. Similar concerns might not be enough to save you.

By making that call, Morris gave himself at least a chance to live. Those of us who are gripped by fear of terrorism and economic difficulties can give ourselves the possibility of a better life as well. The first assignment on Day One entails a quick-writing process. This phase is essential for you to understand your own concerns.

- **Write fast**: Use a pen and paper, or type on a keyboard. As fast as you can write, jot down as many of your fears as you can think of as it relates to terrorism and economic hardship. Once you've written down a particular fear or concern, don't think about it too much. Keep busy jotting down one fear after another.

- **List plenty**: List every fear that comes to mind, as fast as it comes to your head. Be as general or as specific as your mind tells you is necessary. Whether your fears are such things as "getting killed by a nuclear bomb" or "not being able to travel anymore," list even things that might seem embarrassing. You're the only person who'll see this, unless you choose to show the list to others.

- **Keep going**: Continue to write, even to the point that you might seem to be getting creative or pushing the edge. If your genuine fears are for the well being of the children of Afghanistan or Iraq, put those things down as well. Mean-hearted worries are game for this list too, such as "I fear we won't kill enough terrorists," or "I fear that greedy corporate executives who caused this financial turmoil will never go to prison."

- **End list**: After one hour is up, stop writing. Or, if you've become exhausted with the process and shut down earlier, that's okay. The idea is to get as many of your fears listed as you can during a relatively short period. If there still are concerns that you didn't have time to list, don't worry. The task here is to form an initial point of reference.

If you're afraid to write anything down, and you still don't have a list, that's OK. You've put yourself in that rare breed that refuses to face or acknowledge their fears under any circumstances. By continuing to follow this lesson, though, you'll understand the importance of such acknowledgements. If you refuse or fail to make a list, unlike mail worker Thomas Morris Jr., you will not have tried to face your concerns. You will not have given yourself a chance at a better life, and in some cases a chance to survive.

Those who've finished their lists realize it gets inner sensations out in the open, and to some degree it was probably even a bit fun. Even folks who found no inkling of joy in making such personal revelations might soon recognize the initial value of this process. Perhaps your list is much shorter than you had envisioned, or maybe it's far longer than you would have dreamed possible.

Now, those who have lists should start reading them. Understand that just because you've written something down doesn't necessarily make it "real" or "permanent." An initial read-through might bring a realization that some newfound worries give you more concern than what just recently caused the worst worry.

Here's the grade so far for those who listed their fears: **A+**

And here's the grade so far for those who didn't list any, whether out of indifference or fear of undergoing such a process: **A+**

Everyone passes. In life, under a democracy and in many cases under dictatorships, many decisions are our own to make. Choose what's right for you. And once again we ask a question that can't possibly be repeated enough: ***Will you choose fear?***

Second Assignment, Your List Review

TV cameras captured images of Afghan children running through the desert. Dozens or hundreds of youngsters scurried from their homes, many of them orphans. Kids reportedly as young as 5 years old walked barefoot for many miles just to get small bags of food dropped as "humanity" packages by the U.S. military. Like it or not, these children were forced to face any potential or "real" fears in order to survive.

Some kids carried bagfuls of these food packets home to their starving families. The food had been dropped in the wilderness during the night by military aircraft. News reports indicated lots of these children were responsible for the survival of their younger siblings, some as young as 1, 2 or 3 years old. Babies fended for themselves amid the heart of war, some of them overcoming even intrinsic fears that can plague the very young.

In many ways, all of us adults have the same hearts and souls that we possessed as children. Certainly only a tiny portion of us ever had to endure such struggles. Today as you face fears of terrorism and financial hardship, you are in a sense a child as well. You're learning or "re-learning" truisms that intrinsically you've already known.

With this in mind, now, it's time to carefully read your list of fears. As you scan, notice that many fears have similarities, such as areas of survival. These initial things might entail questions like whether you'll die or if you'll have enough to eat and maintain good health. Look for these attributes, and do the following for each.

X-Mark: Mark an "X" beside all fears that mean physical death. These range from your own murder at the hands of terrorists or starvation due to corporate greed, due to the loss of loved ones or co-workers. Elimination of food sources, contamination of drinking water and nuclear attacks are the kinds of things that fall in this category.

Y-Mark: Mark a "Y" beside fears that could damper or curtail your lifestyle. These cover such occurrences as gasoline supplies being dried up, forcing you to walk instead of drive. Aging too quickly due to worry, or the destruction of America's entertainment media like cable TV, could fall within this category as well.

Z-Mark: Jot a "Z" beside worries of potential losses that might occur outside your sphere of living. Things like "I'm afraid thousands more people will be killed," or "I'm afraid many innocent people will die in Iraq, Afghanistan, Pakistan and the Middle East."

Zero-Mark: Write "Zero" beside all remaining fears that don't yet have symbols by them. These could include miscellaneous items, such as "I fear that if I worry about terrorism or economic hardship too much, I'll forget to brush my teeth in the morning." Don't be embarrassed if you have a lot of "zeroes." Plenty of our fears are difficult to understand.

Scan your Grading System

Now, review each category. Most of your "X" worries are deadly or harmful things that will happen to you anyway, no matter what you do—unless you're an integral part of the government or industry. "Y" worries represent more "helpless" situations, outcomes that never could cause you major physical harm. If "Z" concerns occurred, life would become as "hassle" compared to how you've known it. And under a "zero" scenario, you'd have to put up with needless inconveniences.

Once you've acknowledged these fears, and even fears that you've refused to admit, REMEMBER NONE OF THEM WILL EVER GO AWAY. Your fears will remain, no matter what you do. You can "kill" your fears, obliterate them in your mind. Even if that happens, though, your fears still exist—except that they would be "bodies or carcasses" of what you've eliminated.

To successfully manage and "control" your fears of terrorism and of economic hardship, you must realize and acknowledge this at all times. If and when you "kill" your fears, they'll still be there within your heart. It's almost as if dead muscle in your aorta, while the overall organ still keeps pumping to keep you alive. You'll learn to "kill" fears by obliterating them in your mind, but like soldiers shot in battle their bodies never go away easily. You can bury your fears or burn them, but there will still be ashes of sorts—proverbial dust that can get into your eyes.

Here's an exclamation that you're an innocent child, a mature adult and a fragile senior citizen all rolled up into one. Your mind controls the emotions of each: the curiosity of the baby, learning to grown and understand; the seasoned wisdom, knowing the difference between what's truly right and wrong for your personality; and the "old" fragile self, realizing it eventually will die—while needing assistance from the youthful child and the Wise One in order to "go" with dignity at the time of your choice.

E pluribus unum ~ out of many, one!

Without necessarily realizing it, throughout your adult life you've worked to earn arrows—or at least images of them. These depictions you labored hard to get appear identical to weapons used by Native Americans or other warriors for thousands of years. After earning these arrow images, you put them in your pocket or even convert them into your bank account. These pointy objects, of course, are on the Great Seal of the United States on $1 bills.

Held by the eagle's left claw, 13 arrows are grasped in a bundle of great strength. They symbolize the "power of unity" and national defense. You might also recall this eagle's right claw grasps an olive branch, which symbolizes the power of peace.

As you master your control of fear against terrorism, corporate greed and selfish politicians, your mind literally serves the same functions as the Great Seal. Thoughts which you control determine your strength, necessary to get past fears that never die even after you've "killed" them. Forever vigilant and on guard to uphold your personal values, your mind also enables you to remain placid and peaceful when the time is "ripe."

Adding even more vigor, your heart helps bring passion to the mind. Your heart becomes an American bald eagle upward in flight, its wings pointed down. Needless to say, a sound mind and heart bring the possibility of freedom from fear.

116

Mindful of these powers, look at your list of fears. Notice once again that many potential outcomes remain unpredictable. Others will happen no matter what, such as the fact you'll die, or that you'll lose most of your loved ones if you live long enough.

Because you're human and vulnerable, you might fear being unable to cope with certain outcomes. Since the Great Seal within your being and within your soul is resilient, there's a realization deep down that "things" happen outside your control. Yet there's an inner strength. Some psychologists believe many of your worries were learned as a child, partly from your environment or from your parents.

Numerous experts in the human psyche also have studied identical twins, concluding that their similar behaviors are likely caused by biology. Certainly, then, let's assume some people have more natural inclination to bravery than others. Even if that's the case, it doesn't take away the fact you can control your mind.

To those who argue you're unable to change because you "cannot teach an old dog new tricks," remember great strides have been made by people in their 20s, 30s, 40s and beyond.

Famed former professional boxing referee Mills Land had plenty of experience in the ring into his 20s as an amateur and as a professional. It wasn't till Lane's 40s that he "blossomed" in other areas of confidence, becoming a world-famous judge and celebrity.

President Abraham Lincoln was despondent as a young man, partly due to the loss of a girlfriend. Lincoln evolved into a far stronger man than some of his acquaintances thought possible.

You might not have anywhere near the wisdom of Lincoln, and perhaps you've never had to fight the way Mills Lane did. But you're just as "human" and capable as these gentlemen.

To evolve like a caterpillar into a butterfly takes nothing more than time and determination. In fact, many experts in motivation tell us that continual change and development in the human condition is not only likely—it's natural.

Some widows discover they depended "too much" on their husbands. Left alone, these women must endure varying degrees of struggle in order to achieve what they consider a sense of normalcy. To be sure, economic woes outside your control have caused you to feel discomfort and apprehension about both the present and the future.

Even so, from these revelations take comfort in knowing you can confront all anxieties on this, the first day of your Fears List. At the moment, if you remain particularly afraid of flying or of spending money, don't worry because you're still in the caterpillar stage. Inside, you have hidden butterfly wings that'll enable you to fly in spirit, even if you still choose to avoid airliners.

During the height of his boxing fame during the 1960s and 1970s, former heavyweight champ Muhammad Ali proclaimed he could "float like a butterfly, and sting like a bee." Although ravaged by disease in his later years, Ali refused to allow the natural shutdown of his human body to destroy the spirit. And while in his 60s, Judge Mills Lane used his personal motto, "Let's Get It On!"—even after suffering a debilitating stroke.

These men learned to trust instinctive reactions. You might not be a fighter, or violent, or feisty, or full of vigor. Still, remember your mind and heart are identical to the Great Seal. Within you rests more than a mere symbol. As author Thomas Haynes Bayly wrote in the early 1800s: "I'd be a butterfly born on a bower, where roses and lilies and violets meet."

Not All Butterflies Are Free

Lisa Beamer, widow of Todd Beamer—the doomed jet passenger who defiantly said, "Let's roll" against terrorists—became a "butterfly" 38 days after the Attack on America. She flew coast-to-coast, taking the same flight schedule on which her husband died. She traveled on Oct. 19, 2001, to show Americans they shouldn't give into fear. If anyone might have cause for concern it was Lisa, mother of two young children at the time while expecting a third the following January.

Wrongly labeled "the weaker sex" for millenniums, the female gender has been tough during this ordeal, from the terrorist attacks well into the economic crisis. Sure, many tears have been shed, and more likely will fall, yet women have been an integral part of our battle team every step of the way. True to the notion that men and women are from different planets, both genders face unique concerns.

Suffice it to say everyone feels challenged to varying degrees. Some women might feel overwhelmed, frustrated by an apparent inability to express deep-felt emotions during such stressful times. A number of men have been just as stunned in fearing the worst for their families. For all involved, there is no need to gain unfound power, for it's already there.

For instance, look at your fear list. Notice that many activities that give fright due to terrorism *could* be enjoyed or endured. You have the *ability* to take a jet flight, although you allow fears to prevent you from doing that. You have the *ability* to open the mail, although you allow fears of anthrax to prevent you from doing that. And you have the *ability* to travel to New York City, although you allow fears to prevent you from doing that thinking of it as a "target." The potential list in this regard could possibly flow for many more pages than you've already written.

For instance, in separate interviews on CNN during the months following the 2008 presidential election, former President Bill Clinton and billionaire Bill Gates predicted the economic recovery would be slow. What if they were right? What if the situation worsened before it improved?

According to "Forbes," foreclosures reached 1.8 million the first half of 2008, already surpassing the 1.5 million foreclosures in all of 2007—and the pattern was expected to worsen with 3 million foreclosures during 2009. Imagine the amount of potential worry you can generate, fearing this negative financial ripple effect could adversely impact your life—if it hasn't already.

The point is clear that each of us has the strength, power and *ability* to do such things if we want. Unless we're physically disabled to the point we're immobile or lack adequate short-term financial resources, the power is within us to move past our notions of what we should be afraid of—if we set our minds to that.

In fact, you have so many choices, you could—if you wanted—behave to the point of being "unreasonable." It's possible to take these strengths to the extreme. Imagine jumping off a building if you're afraid of heights or actively trying to kill suspected terrorists yourself if you're untrained and unauthorized to do such things. For this reason, keep your value system in mind.

Being careful to remember basic principles entrusted by your powerful arrows and peaceful olive branch, start scanning the list from one item to another. Take note that you actually *could* do many or all the things you listed. Examples: you *could* drive near nuclear power plants although you're terrified terrorists might attack them; you *could* spend $25 more on groceries this week than budgeted if you have the money, although you're afraid you'll get laid off from work next week; and you *could* buy extra copies of this book for fearful friends, although you're afraid they might criticize you for giving such a unique gift.

Furthermore, the worst of the dangers or possibilities listed here might be taken to the extreme, for you *could* die in a terrorist attack or from starvation after becoming homeless. You *could*, if you're young enough, end up being drafted, fighting in this war, or losing your job due to an economic slump caused by corporate greed.

The question rests on what you want, and whether you're willing to push your behavior past certain worries and not others. Now that the point has been driven home of your widespread powers, you'll need to learn to use them.

It's almost as if you're Superman shortly after arriving on Earth for the first time. Those are among attributes that make this comic book hero a Man of Steel.

"Forget Your Troubles?"

Audiences cheered wildly whenever Judy Garland belted, "Forget your troubles, come on get happy … throw all your fears away … Forget your troubles, come on get happy—get ready for the judgment day!"

Well, like it or not amid the wars on terrorism and economic crisis, we're all floating down a river toward certain outcomes. Finding happiness surely might not be a cup of tea, or a "Good Ship Lolly Pop," like the craft made famous by child star Shirley Temple in the 1930s.

Yet at the start of your three-day learning process, "throwing away" your fears is unbelievably as easy as singing such tunes! In fact, getting rid of your fears is far simpler than singing, even if you don't know how to carry a tune.

Here's your next assignment: This very moment, grab the list of fears that you jotted down, and immediately throw that paper into the garbage can! That's right, stop reading here for a second, pick up your entire list, and put it in the nearest trash can in your home or office.

What!? You might say, and you probably are, why should I take my list of fears that I'm supposed to learn to "attack, and to manage" and then do something as crazy as throwing it away? "I refuse to do it! I want these fears, so I can keep reading them and facing them."

However, whatever your reaction, stop arguing now and toss your list into the trash at this very moment!

There, now. Doesn't it make you feel better? Your fears are gone, aren't they? Everything's all right?

After tossing your fears away, all of them, into the trash, you realize the list is gone—but all your fears remain! Or are they!

"What if I can't remember what I'm supposed to be afraid of?" you might ask, worried. "How am I expected to remember everything on my list, as these lessons continue?! **I can't remember everything I'm afraid of, on a moment's notice! I can't remember everything I'm supposed to be afraid of! This isn't fair!"**

As we've already made clear, life isn't necessarily "fair." For you, throwing fears in your trashcan was either easy to accomplish or it wasn't. In fact, at this very moment, if you haven't already actually thrown away your First Day Fear List, please stop a moment and do it now. This isn't a "mind game" or a trick question. Or, then again, is it?

"Can I really throw fears away that easily?" you ask. "I know my fears are still there. My fears are still on that paper I wrote, if I haven't burned it already. And my fears are all still in my head and they're still in my heart, even if I can't remember them! How dare these lessons try to trick me, for I can't throw all my fears away! My fears are still with me, I think."

Yes, you've got it right, your fears are still within you. And those same fears are on paper, in your garbage can as well.

Your fears are where you put them. You see you're in control. Your mind easily can shuffle your fears, and put them where you want them. Each fear is still there, and still "real." When you first got each fear it became "real" because you enabled your environment and then your mind to "make" it that way.

As you've seen, from the course of reading just a single page you've managed to "get rid" of all the fears of terrorism and economic hardship that you could possibly think of within one hour. But what if you can't remember them now?

Well, rest easy in knowing that your conscious mind and subconscious minds will never forget those fears. And now that you know your fears can be "moved" to where you want them, there's a possibility you'll be able to quickly discover where to move these sensations within your mind and heart.

Of course, moving your fears from the "front" of your mind to the "back" of your mind will not make them go away. Just as important, managing your fears by denying them or thinking of other things will never prevent them from healing your heart.

Still, take comfort in knowing that the ***ability*** to move your fears is a vital step, a necessary step in managing them. Because you have the ***ability*** to make that happen, your fears never can control you—***for now you know that you control your fears***. Remember what we've described about ***abilities***? Well, you're capable of moving your fears.

Think of it, in a sense, like cleaning up the files on your desktop. You can move files into drawers, and throw unwanted documents away. As you've seen, the initial phase of learning to "move" your fears was easy; now, it's time to put your worries where you want them.

Meantime, if you're one of those who never made a list in the first place, you've already saved yourself some effort. You never had to go through the hassle of compiling the lists, because *even if you've refused to face your fears, you don't need to acknowledge all of them in order for such concerns to go away. In choosing not to make a list, if that had been your decision, you were the "master" of your emotions. In refusing to complete the assignment, you already see the Power of your convictions. You are strong! Like all of us, you have a mighty mind!*

Well, at this phase on Day One, all participants—even those who refused to make a list—and those who declined to throw their lists away can take delight in learning that everyone gets an **A+**.

The Heart of the Statue of Liberty

By the time U.S. President Grover Cleveland accepted the Statue of Liberty on behalf of the United States in 1886, the symbol had become famous worldwide. Entitled "Liberty Enlightening the World," this gift from France at Liberty Island in New York Harbor welcomed millions of immigrants for decades to come.

As the War on Terrorism and the battle to improve the economy intensifies, words on Lady Liberty's tablet remain emblazoned on the world psyche: "Give me your tired, your poor, your huddled masses yearning to breathe free, the wretched refuse of your teeming shore. Send these, the homeless, tempest-tost to me, I lift my lamp beside the golden door!"

Without necessarily realizing it, your mind works as a vacuum cleaner sucking up every bit of info. In much the way that Lady Liberty welcomed immigrants, your mind has assimilated unimaginable amounts of data. Controversy abounds on how well America has handled new immigrants. Your mind is the same with info.

Some critics complain that especially in recent decades, America has shut out potential immigrants while welcoming others. Your mind behaves the same way, deciding which information to recall while discarding other data as worthless or unrecognizable. In this sense a statue of individualism stands within each of us.

Accepting this famous sculpture on behalf of the USA, President Cleveland proclaimed that "We will not forget that liberty made here her home, nor shall her chosen alter be neglected." Embracing similar commitment, it's essential to remain vigilant in processing information your mind receives.

"There is no repose for the mind except in the absolute; for feeling, except in the infinite; for the soul, except in the divine," Swiss-born philosopher Henri Frédéric Amiel wrote in his journals begun in 1847. Indeed, the brain is a universal black hole, blasting some info into the ether and making other data paramount in priority.

Sigmund Freud, the father of psychoanalysis, reportedly exclaimed, "Knowledge is the intellectual manipulation of carefully verified observations." Whether cognizant of this or not, the brain scans all data and recognizes it, with many automatic reactions set into place during early childhood.

If it's true what Freud assumed, "thought is action in rehearsal," there's still opportunity for each of us to change and modify our reactions and resulting behaviors. It has been said that "from error to error, one discovers the entire truth." Many fears of terrorism and financial crisis result from mental "mistakes" or misinformation.

Freud was on track in his conclusions that "men are strong only so long as they represent a strong idea. They become powerless when they oppose it." Following a similar course, your brain has the power to guide you in writing down your fears of terrorism and financial hardship; it is just as capable of enabling you to toss those worries into the trashcan.

In his "Arsenal in Springfield" in the 1800s, Henry Wadsworth Longfellow noted: "Were half the power that fills the world with terror, were half the wealth that bestowed at camps and courts, given to redeem the human mind from error, there were no need for arsenals and forts."

Heralded as "the greatest daredevil in history," Evel Knievel earned his way into "Guinness Book of World Records" after suffering more broken bones than anyone—surviving to tell about his adventures—till his death by natural causes in 2007 at age 69. Knievel set limits for his actions, breaking barriers for what he considered reasonable stunts.

Facing terrorism and economic adversity, your key assignments entail areas of behavior where you now feel comfortable—and expanding actions into new areas. There's no need to behave in the style of Knievel to overcome most concerns. Avoid taking unnecessary deadly or physically harmful actions just to prove a point.

At the heart of this phase, consider your level of what many psychologists call "comfort zones." These are actions where you feel safe or unthreatened. For example, consider Mister Fear, whose worries of terrorism and financial strife limit his monthly entertainment budget to $20. Prior to the Attack on America and severe economic recession, he had spent $500 monthly for entertainment.

By gradually feeling more at ease and unthreatened, he started spending $45, and then $75, and then higher. Mister Fear began to re-enter comfort zones he had enjoyed in the past. In similar fashion, by deciding how far he was willing to jump with his motorcycle during stunts, Knievel set his own comfort zones. Each time the famous daredevil went further, he expanded his degree of comfort. *Yet every time they expand their behaviors into new or expanded "comfort zones," daredevils, soldiers and everyday folk like you still have fear. Even many of the world's greatest daredevils and generals have admitted that during their most "death-defying" actions they remained terrified.*

As your mind serves as a Lady Liberty, processing data on terrorism, you will always have fear. Entering Day Two of your 3REST™ lessons, realize there's no need to cross the threshold of what you consider reasonable. *Yet the only way to break through your current comfort zone and enter new areas of comfort is to SIMPLY DO THEM.*

Remember that as he entered World War I, Sergeant York never felt comfortable with the notion of killing others. His battlefield heroics enabled him to break through that moral challenge, partly out of a need to save his fellow soldiers and to win existing battles.

In "simply doing it" to expand your behaviors into new areas of comfort, you're almost like Sergeant York who survived and even like Amelia Earhart who became lost and presumable dead during her round-the-world flight attempt in 1937.

In breaking barriers of fear or concern in entering marriage, Earhart wrote to her future husband, George Palmer Putnam, before their 1931 wedding: "I must extract a cruel promise, and that is you will let me go in a year if we find no happiness together." Earhart set a comfort zone in her personal life, just as she took a calculated risk in aviation that resulted in her disappearance.

Threatened by economic problems and terrorism, during Day Two of 3REST™ lessons you'll begin the process of setting your own boundaries, determining comfort zones and "killing" fears—although you realize and accept the fact they'll always remain. Your mind is the Statue of Liberty, the rifle held by Sergeant York, the motorcycle on which Evel Knievel rode and the pen Earhart used to write her letters.

During Day One, you were essentially in pre-flight training, learning basics of how to soar. During Day Two, you'll study and understand your "aircraft," the mind, and discover its operations before, during and after flights. And in Day Three, it'll be time to take off on a solo flight and roar just like a Stealth Bomber into clouds that have been your fears of economic hardship and terrorism.

CHAPTER TWELVE

3REST™ ~ Day 2 Lessons Begin

U.S. Military planes zoomed off aircraft carriers, launching continual attacks during initial months after the Attack on America. Pilots shot "daisy bombs" and "smart bombs" at intended targets, sometimes unintentionally hitting innocent people. Using every technology in their arsenal remained vital.

As Day Two begins, you're going to "learn to be a pilot." You probably didn't realize such training was necessary to conquer fears. Yet your pilot training remains on track. First, we'll introduce you to the cockpit, all available controls there—plus a review of the limitations and abilities of your aircraft.

American fighter pilots in the wars in Iraq and Afghanistan often zoom many hundreds of miles per hour, approaching or surpassing the speed of sound. Your aircraft is faster, sleeker and even more agile than theirs, with countless turning and maneuvering capabilities. Military fighter pilots must take orders from their superiors; you're the boss of your own jet.

Your "aircraft" in this case is your mind. You'll need it in order to blast through fears and conduct activities you desire. At the start, it's helpful to review numerous comparisons between American jet fighters and your Mind-Jet aircraft. First, military jets cost millions of dollars, while your Mind-Jet is free.

You were born with this Mind-Jet and started "flying" it as a toddler. Because many of your reactions as a Mind-Jet pilot are instinctive, it's helpful to review what's in the cockpit so you can learn and review how to take off, maneuver and land. Both Mind-Jets and U.S. Military Stealth Bombers have pilot seats.

Like pilots in military aircraft, you must accept responsibility for everything that happens in your Mind-Jet and for how it's flown. In some ways, the military pilots have a much easier job than you. That's because flying is their primary assignment. Your chores include mechanics and maintenance.

In the military, well-trained mechanics check out and repair aircraft each time they're flown. Many aircraft maintenance duties are completed while pilots rest; worn-out parts are replaced and expensive fluids installed. By comparison, you control your Mind-Jet by feeding it with info before and during missions.

Numerous other comparisons are necessary, before you begin your first training flight. Carefully review the following cockpit equipment list, because understanding these basics will be essential during your fight against fears of terrorism and economic hardship. Even after your initial three-day training, you might want to occasionally review these points:

- **Pre-Flight Checks:** Both military and civilian flyers of actual aircraft must review a pre-flight list before takeoff. This includes navigation, a study of the weather, and determining destinations. Such reviews are unavoidable during Mind-Jet travel. Nonetheless, if possible before departure, it's a good idea to decide or determine where you're willing to go.
- **Weather conditions:** Before taking off, standard jet pilots review weather conditions. This is done to determine the amount of fuel needed, to see if an alternate route is necessary, and to decide whether to cancel a flight. For Mind-Jets, "bad weather" arises in the form of danger such as information on a pending attack or an upcoming job loss.

- **Responsibility**: In military aircraft, pilots are primarily responsible for missions—while many assistants such as runway workers and radar control personnel take heat as well. As a Mind-Jet pilot, you must be ready to take all heat without blaming others, since you're the only person making decisions.
- **Navigation:** Some military aircraft have navigators aboard other than pilots. By contrast, as a Mind-Jet pilot, you're in charge of deciding for yourself where to go and how to get there. News reports, advice from friends, word-of-mouth, and education are among a Mind-Jet's best navigational resources.
- **Control tower:** While attacking terrorists, military pilots have control towers and computers to help guide them. Mind-Jet pilots must rely on instincts and reactions, except in cases where they accomplish things as part of teams or in casual groups. For both types of pilots such assistance from others can be vital.
- **Radio communication:** Standard jet pilots depend greatly on radio communications; they listen to each other and to control personnel. At least in some ways, Mind-Jet pilots are far different; it's often essential for them to avoid dwelling on mindless babble or "thoughts" that slow them down.

Review your comparisons, and realize similarities between yourself and military aircraft are not all that far-fetched. Used as a learning tool to help bring your efforts into focus, these situations can be employed to determine progress. In fact, in a creative sense, your Mind-Jet can travel in many more ways than a military jet.

Your Mind-Jet can serve as a submarine, diving under the water or out of sight when you want to deny or ignore a situation. By contrast, the only ways for a standard jet pilot to hide is to eject chaff to confuse heat-seeking missiles, land, outrun pursuers, trick radars through stealth maneuvers, or shoot the enemy.

Determine your attack, escape or travel routes

Standard jet pilots have no option other than to eject during certain mechanical failures. The Mind-Jet pilot is far superior, because his aircraft doesn't have structural or engineering limitations such as those in standard jets. All humans have creative abilities that can help get them out of jams.

Consider Apollo 13, which sustained severe oxygen system problems while en route to the moon. Scientists on Earth brainstormed. Thanks to creativity and teamwork, they developed a solution that saved its astronauts from almost certain death.

Many years later, Apollo 13 Commander Jim Lovell was asked what psychological, physiological or physical changes he underwent after his moon mission: "I do not worry about crisis anymore."

Capt. George Burk, critically injured in a 1970 military jet crash in which he was the only survivor, suffered multiple injuries and extensive burns but later became a motivational speaker. The Adrian Daily Telegram in Adrian, Mich., quoted Burk's talk to schoolchildren: "Stop with the 'would,' the 'could,' the 'should.' Re-script the 'shall,' 'will,' 'must.' Don't let anyone tell you that you can't. Tell them that you can, you will, and you shall."

Another motivational speaker, Vietnam War veteran and ex-Marine Tom Shugure was on the 34th floor of Tower II at the World Trade Center on Sept. 11, 2001. President of Carolina Capital Markets, Inc., Shugrue was there for an 8 a.m. business meeting scheduled to last 30 minutes. He was admiring the view at 8:45 a.m., when a hijacked aircraft hit Tower I.

Shugrue took charge of a military-style sweep of the floor to ensure everyone there was safe and prepared to evacuate. And then he decided *to go back and get his briefcase.*

"One part of me said, 'Don't be stupid, don't go back and get my briefcase,'" Shugrue told the News Observer in North Carolina. "Another part of me says, 'Wait a minute, I need it for my 10 o'clock meeting.'

"When you're in a crisis situation, or war zone or something like this, are you going to think about tomorrow? No. You're thinking about right now. You see, I was thinking '10 o'clock meeting.'"

Instinctively as pilots of their own proverbial Mind-Jet aircraft, humans are always up in the air—always forced to make decisions. When terrifying situations suddenly strike, we must make the best choices we can—usually based on our values.

Shugrue's actions immediately after the jet hit can be considered a heroic example of how personal values come to play in terrorist attacks or in severe economic crisis: first, he considered the needs and safety of others; second, he addressed what he considered as his personal need; and third, he finally left the building.

Such situations have many possible outcomes partly because values differ. Some people in Shugrue's shoes might have got the heck out of the building right away, ignoring the safety of others, and losing all memories of the suitcase or business needs.

As the proverbial pilot of your own mind, you'll be making choices— "right" or "wrong"—no matter what situation should arise. And now that you're more fully cognizant of these scenarios than you may have been before, you're ready to inspect your mind.

Once the initial review is completed, your eventual assignments will be to "kill" certain fears. When that occurs, there's no turning back as your mental jet approaches supersonic speed.

Scare Headlines Roar into Your Mind!

"Scare" headlines shot into the human psyche in late 2008, as the holiday season clicked into gear a few months after the severe international economic meltdown kicked into full gear. TV news anchors, radio talk hosts, and newspaper headlines blared that we're depressed, terrified and that we wanted to stay home.

Similar outcomes prevailed as the holidays approached seven years earlier in 2001. "Remember when it was the good old days, when it was the Grinch who stole Christmas?" asked a front-page headline in "USA Today." Such headlines make fear "real" in the minds of many, and terror or fear spread. "This year, it's terrorists who threaten to rob us of the holiday. No matter how hard Americans try, it won't be quite the jolly Christmas yore."

"Even at the mall, I look around more now," one worried shopper at Fashion Center in Pentagon City told the newspaper. "I realize this could be a good target for terrorists."

In the wake of the financial downfall and of the terrorist attack, journalists everywhere reported that the recent crisis had affected everything from shopping to parties to mailing. In late 2001, the use of cars to take short trips soared as terrified holiday celebrants avoided air travel. Initial reports indicated many holiday shoppers were taking their gift lists online, to buy on the Net rather than visit malls.

Both in 2001 and in 2008, "Bah! Humbug!" roared the collective consciousness of the USA, as if everyone had suddenly become an Ebenezer Scrooge. "What right have you to be merry? What reason have you to be merry? You're poor enough?"

In the famous tale "A Christmas Carol" by Charles Dickens, Scrooge's nephew asks him to give a reason for such grumpiness and gloom during the holidays.

"What else can I be?" Scrooge replied, behaving the way many Americans became before and after the holidays. "When I live in such as world of fools as this? Merry Christmas! Out upon merry Christmas!"

Ghosts that never existed began haunting Americans and people everywhere. Consumers, potential travelers and some sports enthusiasts allowed tainted media hype to contaminate and damage their proverbial Mind-Jet engines. Of course, real and present terrorist threats continued to exist.

Remember, no standard jet pilot is allowed to get his aviation license if he's too scared to fly or overly apprehensive. Sitting in a pilot's seat is no place for a mentally deranged flyer. And yet as human beings, at least in the Mind-Jet sense, we must "fly" in order to exist; it's a natural and mandatory part of our nature.

Retired U.S. astronaut Buzz Aldrin, veteran of the first successful moon-walk mission in 1969, once told an interviewer of his natural reaction during that first lunar stroll: "From the distance of the moon, Earth was four times the size of a full moon to see from Earth. It was a brilliant jewel in the black velvet sky. Yet it was still at a great distance, considering the challenge of the voyage home."

Amid struggles to overcome their natural fears, people everywhere can see blessings—the "diamond in the rough"—if they allow themselves to view positive possibilities. For many of us life's most joyful experiences occur when we overcome challenges—to push ourselves beyond the "limits" of what we once thought possible.

Frank Shorter, 1972 Olympic gold medal marathon winner, mustered up enough confidence to write the script for the hit movie "Love Story" starring Ryan O'Neal. Later, Shorter underwent back surgery, but refused to let that slow him down. Shorter told an interviewer he quickly began to exercise after going under the knife.

"When I go back in for a follow-up, they'll see if the bone has fused—which I'm sure it has," the ever-confident Shorter told the interviewer. "Then, we'll start range-of-motion stuff, and probably in another six weeks I start to run. I started biking already."

On the West Coast of America, a perennially positive attitude brought a noted newspaper writer from the brink of death—beginning about the day of the Attack on America. After Reno Gazette-Journal Columnist Rollan Melton's health steadily deteriorated in a six-week period, his family began to accept the fact that he would not survive.

By the 9th and 10th of September, 2001, Melton's body—ravaged by congestive heart failure, had wilted into the form of an old, rotting leaf. Yet seemingly on the day of the attack, Melton's health began to improve as relatives told him what happened. At age 70, he began to sit up in bed, watch news reports on the new war, and refused to entertain negative thoughts or comments about his own health.

Within two months, Melton—whom many people were sure would not survive through September—was up and out of bed, visiting restaurants several nights each week. He retained his ability to laugh, and to ask thoughtful questions of his many friends. Asked if worries about his family had generated his increase in vigor, Melton said he didn't know.

In fact, as father of this publication's author, Melton became the first person to read the initial draft of the book that you're reading now, and he fully approved—reading it, cover-to-cover, he said, at least twice by mid-December 2001.

Throughout his ordeal, Melton refused to allow negative thoughts to bring him down, even till he died in his sleep of natural causes on Jan. 13, 2002. A similar positive attitude had been credited with bringing Melton success in business, in his writing career and family life as well.

It's the same brand of positive attitude that still can strengthen America and the world as we all face terrorism and economic plight. Our thoughts supply the primary fuel for our Mind-Jets.

Embrace the concept of positive thinking, and make it reality. Turn all negative thoughts around into potential positives. That's an effective way to get your behavior on course toward conquering fear. Creative vision usually can result in positive outcomes.

By collectively convincing ourselves the economy is destined for gloom, it'll become that. By having everyone believe we're all doomed to die in an attack, we'll decrease chances of taking action necessary to defend ourselves. The sister concepts of gloom and doom are no match for the notion that knowledge is power.

In 1910, more than two decades after Thomas Edison invented motion pictures, there were some folks who noted movies hadn't necessarily caught on as the most accepted entertainment medium.

"It will revolutionize the stage," the ever-positive and inquisitive Edison insisted. "The future of the motion picture in the amusement line will be in the form of a combination between it and the phonograph."

Blessed with a non-stop work ethic, Edison created his vision of "talkies" many years before they reached the big screen. In this War on Terrorism and economic hardship, adopting similar positive attitudes can enable each of us to plan and achieve a bright future. To do otherwise is to fail, for the enemy will rarely falter in its convictions.

At age 39 in 1921, future U.S. President Franklin Delano Roosevelt was on vacation at Campobello Island when stricken by polio. He spent the next seven years trying to recover the use of his legs. Then, he launched his successful presidential campaign, and went on the lead America to victory in World War II.

Although stricken by severe illness from effects of a massive stroke, President Woodrow Wilson remained undaunted and as relentless as possible in the last 18 months of his presidency.

There's no need to be an Edison, a Roosevelt, a Shorter or a Wilson in order to persevere. Everyday folk across America already have shown boundless resilience in the face of economic hardship. As is the case in any battle or controversy, there will always be negative thinkers. Such people strive to beat down those who have positive visions, telling them such dreams are impossible.

Racists taunted Jackie Robinson, as he became the first African American baseball player to enter the major leagues in 1947. Robinson mustered enough courage to perform well at the game, although a target of racism. Maintaining a positive attitude wasn't always easy for Robinson; there were ups and downs, but he persevered—before eventually being inducted into the Major League Baseball Hall of Fame.

"Yes I can! It starts with a dream! It's always too soon to quit!" So said the Web site of Rudy Ruttinger, a famed former Notre Dame football player who struggled to play in at least one game—despite those who said it could never happen due his lack of athletic talent. "Rudy is a true story, and is an unforgettable testament to the power of dreams and the triumph of the common man. Millions have been inspired by his great movie."

The enemies of Robinson, Ruttinger and many others like us are the Terrorists of Negativity. These people will try to tear down your mind, and tell you only the worst outcomes are possible. Whatever they say, there's no denying your mind helps master your destiny. Take charge of your flight. You've got your own wings, your own goals and dreams.

Your mind is yours, and yours alone—so the terrorists and greedy corporations and lobbyists and politicians can be damned if they think otherwise.

Find Your "Golden Spike"

Your ability to "kill" fear is as powerful as the golden spike, driven at Promontory Summit, Utah, in 1869. That ceremony marked the joining of the Union Pacific and Central Pacific railroads, linking the nation's first transcontinental railway system. Those who use their minds to link the Fear Train with the Train of Progress take great strides in winning the battle against political lobbyists and terror.

Legend continues that Central Pacific President Leland Stanford missed the spike on his first swing, striking laughter from the crowd. Many celebrants had driven thousands of spikes to build those rails. Their collective labors made America's expansion possible. They had worked as one.

Terrorists and political lobbyists whose only interests are selfish and self-centered want to strike us all with similar fear. But by being together, we also can ride a rail powered by positive responses. Such success starts with the actions of each individual. Every person can pierce fear through the heart by simply doing what these adversaries want us to avoid.

Proceed knowing that there simply are NO MISTAKES that you can make in this regard. That's because you—and all of us—will succeed when we take action to spend money, fly, meet in public and engage in other activities. And if we survived the same trip with no crashes or incidents, or if we eventually got a good job—as "odds" show we will if persistence prevails—we've learned it can be okay to show little or no fear, and that WE CAN SUCCEED.

It can't be emphasized enough that to do otherwise, to not take such actions is to lose personal freedoms. Outlandish as it might seem, we have a chance to learn even when we fail. And it's by learning that we progress.

Keep in mind that there's no need to be a daredevil, to take unnecessarily great risks—such as buying a plane ticket to Pakistan, asking for a job you might have little chance to get, or announcing to certain people that you "hate their guts." And if you feel no need to take even a miniscule risk, that you might die against tremendous odds doing something, that's your prerogative, too.

Remember that with economic hardship and terrorism, there's great personal risk when making life decisions. Like any standard pilot, in order to reach your destination you must relax, trust intuition and embrace "preferences"—those things you might want to do most. Your Mind-Jet requires such action if you're ever going to progress.

"A man's ingress into the world is naked and bare, his progress through the world is trouble and care," John Edwin wrote in the 1800s. "And lastly, his egress out of the world is nobody knows where. If we do well here, we shall do well there. I can tell you no more if I preach a whole year."

More than two months after the Attack on America, Tom Ridge, at the time the U.S. director of Homeland Security, vowed to seek substantial new spending to fight terrorism. Ridge cited a need for more equipment and additional agents, while upgrading the national health system to respond to biological or chemical attacks.

"We need to be stronger," said Ridge, a former Pennsylvania governor and Vietnam War veteran. "We need to be larger. We need to be better."

Ridge referred to the nation's committed resources and its infrastructure. Individually, pilots of Mind-Jets—specifically those people who are threatened by economic strife and terrorism—also can work to strengthen their internal resources.

Truly, if we want, each of us is filled with the Cowardly Lion of "The Wizard of Oz," which cried "I do believe in ghosts!" Yet there's just as much gumption. Consider the Kabul City Zoo, in a community captured by Afghan rebels two months after the Attack on America.

"Through this war is more of a yawn these days, it was not so long ago when this lion, Marjan, used to be king of Kabul's urban jungle," NBC News reported. "A mujahedeen fighter who had survived combat with the Soviet Army was not so lucky when he jumped into the lion's den to tease the beast. Marjan promptly ate him."

To be sure, just the way Marjan gobbled up this gentleman, you're capable of eating all your fears of economic hardship and of terrorism. That way you can digest them in whatever way you would like. If you want, spit out certain sections you find distasteful, such as the notion of nuclear war. Meantime, you might want to fully digest fears of jet travel or of job loss, and take a flight or look for new employment anyway.

All along, realize that like that tired old lion Marjan, even you can take too many risks. The day after eating the soldier, Marjan was injured when a relative of the dead man threw a hand grenade into its cage. As NBC noted, "When Marjan pounced on it thinking it was food, he lost one eye and 95 percent of his sight in the other."

In appropriate repetition, it has been made clear that you could die or be severely injured or starve in the current crisis. A more frightening possibility is that you'll choose to remain in your cage, trapped for the rest of your life like Marjan. So keep your wits about you, as you hone your Mind-Jet skills and discover the joys of exhilaration in flight.

CHAPTER THIRTEEN

Day 2 ~ Panic Attack

The "sex act" and panic have a lot in common. Both put participants in physical overdrive. Natural reactions overtake those involved. Heartbeats race. Breathing intensifies, to the point it's overwhelming. Perspiration shoots from every pore. Grunting and uncontrollable sounds are sometimes made.

While most sexual activity by humans is consensual, those who undergo panic aren't always overjoyed by such symptoms. When used wisely, a sense of panic and dread can be employed for survival. Terrified people have been known to get "adrenalin rushes," enabling them to lift or push cars from atop accident victims.

Cases of severe panic attack can make people roll around on the ground and curl up into tight balls of human flesh. Physicians, psychiatrists and psychologists handle such cases best. Unless a "victim" of severe panic knows how to control his symptoms the situation sometimes worsens.

Severe panic often results from fear. People unable to cope with terror or fright suffer. Some experts recommend controlling panic by learning how to manage symptoms. Anyone who has ever been horrified during a moment of possible death or severe injury might recall these warning signs.

An effective and relaxed Mind-Jet pilot must learn to control breathing. Such physical management is the most important factor in working through fear. For thousands of years, many of the world's greatest philosophers, physicians and even athletes have realized that the way we breathe dictates our control, enhancing self-awareness.

"Her suffering ended with the day, yet lived she at the close, and breathed the long, long night away in statue-like repose," James Aldrich wrote in his 1800s classic "A Death Bed."

From the beginning of life until the end, breathing is an overriding influence. During the exhaustive labor of childbirth, female mammals breathe slowly at times—while occasionally trying to slow their oxygen intake. Athletes often are taught to grunt as they inhale tremendously large breaths to give them power. Weightlifters, boxers, and football players sometimes "grunt" right before and during impact.

Combatants who are beaten down often lose the ability to control their own breathing rhythms. These victims get out of sync with other necessary physical attributes. Defeat follows. In this world where "Might Makes Right" strives to be the norm, those who battle fear against economic hardship should learn to breathe in a cool, easy manner.

Those who've studied or practiced yoga understand. There's no need to be a Tibetan Monk or Buddhist to realize the benefits of "mindful breathing." Cultures worldwide have embraced and benefited. The body, spirit and mind calm when breathing eases.

Another Day-2 Assignment: Concentrate on your lung reactions and impulses. Take slow, deep, purposeful breaths. Pause momentarily between exhales and inhales. After a few moments there's a realization that to breathe slow, fully, and purposefully brings sensations of relaxation, mindfulness and even sleepiness.

These reactions are the opposite of fear, to be at ease and in control. Cognizant of the great power of breathing, when and if a sudden panic attack occurs, you'll instinctively know to control your breaths. In order to prepare, practice such breathing often.

During today's exercise, as you breathe in slowly remember that your mind is in control. By using your mind, you can control your breathing rate. In fact, this knowledge can save your life if you're severely injured in an attack. If your arm gets shot off or blown apart in an explosion, you might be lucky enough to instinctively remember to breathe slowly in the minutes that follow—if you're still alive.

By training your mind beforehand for that possibility, chances increase that part of you will muster strength to control breathing. Doing so could prevent you from going into shock, a severe reaction that can result in death.

As some mothers know who've trained in pre-childbirth classes, controlled breathing also can assist in helping to sustain people through extreme, sustained periods of severe physical pain. Take this further, and realize that if your relatives, friends and co-workers are killed or injured in a terrorist attack, or if they lose their jobs on a second's notice, it would be natural for you to wail or cry in grief.

Allow controlled breathing at appropriate times to ease you through painful periods. People who've been through the shock or numbness of divorce know that for some it can stifle or constrict breathing. Other severe symptoms such as extensive weight loss follow, just as in war.

Even after this three-day lesson concludes, for many it's an excellent idea to maintain mindful and controlled breathing as an integral part of daily life. Like exercise, which results in extensive breathing over sustained periods, slow breathing can be used as an excellent stress reliever. And it's free.

Other potential symptoms of stress are also harmful as they prevent people from functioning well and from working through situations perceived as fearful. Keep in mind the following primary factors, and practice ways to relieve them. Such exercise before stressful situations could prove beneficial:

- **Rigid, tight muscles:** Anyone who has been "locked in fear" knows the sensation of tightening up, as they become rigid throughout the body. First, breathe slow and steadily to practice loosening up. As this occurs, wiggle your arms, legs and torso. Slowly move your neck around in various directions. Do this for several minutes.
- **Perspiration:** When nerves flare and worry increases, perspiration often covers the body. For the most part, sweating is a good thing in stressful situations because it prevents the body from becoming overheated. For those worried about causing offensive odors, wear loose clothing or light cotton clothes. Dehydration is a possible negative symptom. Drink plenty of fluids during stressful situations.
- **Sights and sounds**: Terror-caused horror sometimes makes it difficult for victims to see or hear well. This can be especially harmful during and immediately after attacks. In today's practice session, slowly roll your eyes around and take a good look at everything around you. Then, listen to every sound your ears capture. By being mindful of your brain's ability to take in such sensations, you can benefit during stressful times.

During the days and weeks to come, it's a good idea to do all these daily exercises. Make them a regular routine, while ensuring that slow breathing techniques are involved. Be good to your body and it'll help your mind, as they continually assist each other. Good, balanced nutrition and exercise are integral to a sense of wholeness.

In "Poor Richard's Almanac" in 1757, Benjamin Franklin printed the famous, "Early to bed and early to rise makes a man healthy, wealthy and wise." Such behaviors might not guarantee richness in the financial sense, but they sure go a long way in making your brain balanced and strong as you fight fears.

"Beware of rashness, but with energy and sleepless vigilance go forward and give us victories," President Abraham Lincoln said in an 1864 letter to Maj. Gen. Joseph Hooker.

Sir Edmund Percival Hillary spent many years of physical and mental preparation before being one of the first two men to stand atop Mount Everest in 1953. Before being slain by an assassin in 1948, Mahatma Gandhi maintained principles of pacifism as he helped lead India to independence in the face of violence. Actor Raymond Burr, best known for his "Parry Mason" TV role, died of liver cancer at age 76 in 1993 after inspiring millions of people with his on-screen abilities to appear calm.

Job candidates going for interviews and employees with difficult bosses have been taught to breathe slowly and to loosen their muscles. By displaying behaviors of people who are relaxed, they often become that, evolving into self assured and confident individuals. Such advice stretches from everyday life to battle situations.

During placid moments and amid battle, a relaxed and successful Mind-Jet pilot breathes in oxygen to the fullest. Such flyers enjoy life to the maximum amount possible. They realize "bad" things can and will happen. Controlling their bodies with their minds enables them to progress.

In a sense, each American is an astronaut in the final 10-second countdown before liftoff. We can prepare to soar into the outer reaches of limitless possibilities. By breathing, relaxing and keeping focused, we're in control and prepared for an uncertain future.

Discretion & Valor

"The better part of valor is discretion," wrote Shakespeare in "Henry IV." Many similar phrases echo this truism. "Valor" sparks images of knights in shining armor. Envision heroes who uphold a solemn creed of honor. To slay a fire-breathing dragon with a mighty sword can refresh the souls of true champions.

Or at least that's the image in common folklore. In order for valor to be graced with emotional value, it must be tempered with "discrimination" or an ability to make responsible decisions. To many, there's nothing wrong—or necessarily admirable, either—in avoiding certain dangers. Such thinking makes it OK to "run like hell" if there's **absolutely** no way to win. Hightail it away if you know your butt is likely to get fried, without any benefit if you decide to continue moving toward the danger.

There's an equally sound argument that "only the brave can be free. Freedom remains expensive, and the price is blood."

Those moral dilemmas serve as a paradox to many who label such situations as "no-win." Ultimately, anyone faced with terrorist threats or horrific economic conditions must decide what's right for himself. There's also the possibility of a draft. Under such forced inscriptions, individual members of the military forces are told what to believe, trained what to believe, and expected what to believe, and ordered how to behave.

As commander of your Mind-Jet, it's up to you to decide how to think, especially if you're not a soldier. Realize many situations have no clear-cut answers. If a factory closes in your neighborhood, many people lucky enough to still hold jobs will have different reactions and responses.

Take time to ponder possibilities. If visions of such atrocities fill you with even more fear, it's essential to use breathing and relaxation methods. Once again, remember to allow yourself to accept that bad things happen and that they will happen.

At this stage, wondering precisely what atrocities might occur isn't as important as developing your primary belief systems. Those who have no values, who care little about anything, are likely to succumb to horror. Realize that what you choose to think may influence your behaviors during attacks, often resulting in outcomes you'll find yourself forced to deal with.

For instance, what if you decide beforehand that it's most important to run like hell during any assault, no matter what the circumstances? Such a decision might result in lifelong guilt, knowing there were children you could have saved but left behind. Conversely, what if you decide you'll fight no matter what the situation? Such a choice might result in regret, knowing you were severely injured when it wasn't necessary to be a hero.

Of course, under both these circumstances you might also end up being OK with no other injuries involved. An effective Mind-Jet pilot soars at all times, accepting results of his decisions no matter what the outcome. To do otherwise is to lose concentration on the fight at hand, resulting in a proverbial mental crash. That tired-but-true phrase "there are no accidents" holds more meaning than ever.

Time For "Brain Washing"

"I'm going to wash that man right out of my hair! I'm going to wash that man right out of my hair!" Mitzi Gaymor sang, in copyrighted lyrics in the hit movie "South Pacific." "I'm going to wash that man right out of my hair, and send him on his way!"

Thank heavens people everywhere realize deep down that they can easily change their minds! "He loves me, he loves me not," while plucking daily pedals happens with little effort. When people allow themselves to get hypnotized, the amazing power of the human mind can work wonders.

"Frankly, my dear, I don't give a damn," barked Rhett Butler to Scarlett O'Hara in the 1939 classic movie "Gone With the Wind." The dashing Butler played by Clark Gable had had enough of Scarlett's ways, and finally changed his mind about wooing her.

Fears of yesterday can become the dreams of tomorrow. Toddlers fearful of riding two-wheel bicycles grow up to enjoy such activity.

Pre-teen boys who've lost confidence suddenly find vigor when they get their first hit in Little League baseball.

Nothing stays the same, and things change. Some have forgotten American fears of Japanese armies and Nazi tanks during World War II. Now, a new generation of fear and concern has stricken the USA, which also will pass with time, replaced by new concerns in the future.

What's one man's junk becomes another fellow's treasure. Some American soldiers who went off to Europe in World War I as teetotalers returned home as seasoned bar hoppers. Young women insecure about physical intimacy sometimes grow to yearn for its pleasures.

In much the same way as these changes evolved, don't be surprised if your mind changes on terrifying issues of today. What might seem like the greatest concern of all time eventually could become what seems like the distant past. Dreams still can come true.

For such basic attitude adjustments, there's no need for the average person to visit psychiatrists or to pay hypnotists. Remember you've been changing your mind always. Danger might remain, but you can easily change your mind again. You always have.

Remember when you enjoyed certain styles of clothes as a child, replaced by far different garments in teen-age years. And adult trends seem to evolve every few years. Even those who are "stuck in their ways" enjoy the blessing of change.

It starts with biology. Every few months your hair needs cutting because it grows. Those who lighten or color their hair must continually upgrade it. Shoes wear out and replacements become necessary. Before long, you can allow worries of financial hardship to "wear out" too."

Rather than wait years or decades for Americans to get over these terrorism fears, we can individually and collectively *change our attitudes as soon as this very moment! Because we control our minds, this very second we can gain such victory*!

First, by saying things aloud they often become "real" in our minds. Teachers of very young children know this, for potential fantasies of toddlers seem limitless. Their possibilities seem great because no one has yet taught them negatives or senseless statements such as: "Dreams really don't come true."

Yes, some children, but not all of them, believe with all their hearts that Santa Claus is real. They know the Easter Bunny is a living creature, and that the Tooth Fairy comes after the loss of a tooth. Those whose parents encourage this are likely to believe.

Today, in guiding your mind in your belief systems about financial strife, you are your own parent! If you're an adult, you are the primary person guiding your belief systems and reactions, both emotional and physical. Take yourself by the hand.

Even people who've never been widely known possess inner strength capable of giving self-guidance. When Greg LeMond of the USA became the first American to win the Tour de France, he did it because he knew he could with assistance from teammates.

When New York City firefighters fashioned a flag pole from rubble at Ground Zero, they did so because they knew they could. Despite understandable trepidations, many postal workers returned to work after Anthrax attacks because they knew they could.

Indeed, the famous Little Train That Could mentioned earlier remains ready at the station for us all. "We can't" is soundly replaced by "we can" and "we are" and "we will" all across the USA every day.

There's something positive in between those gloomy headlines. From the perspective of many Americans, voters made President Obama's campaign slogan, "Yes We Can!" a reality, making him the nation's first black president.

Death, destruction and dastardly deeds make newspaper front pages and top TV stories before "happy news." Yet it's positive attitudes that keep food going into grocery stores so we can eat, and that help motivate electric utility personnel to keep our lights on.

Negative occurrences in those months after the severe economic meltdown remained unavoidable. Record unemployment, a sagging nationwide and international economy, and dismal travel industry business gave many people heartaches. The pain of no paychecks left many in tears.

Dismal, woeful memories of recent layoffs—coupled by bailouts for some of the same banks that helped cause the financial crisis—left many Americans stunned and in a state of shock. Such statements might seem like little solace now, but remember, similar calamities have happened before on a massive scale, and they'll likely happen again in coming decades or centuries.

The sufferings of many people overshadow beliefs that "to thine own self be true" wins out every time. Unbendable knowledge remains that we can change our minds. We have always changed our minds, and we are doing it again in fighting to make the depressed economy rebound. Some people on the verge of divorcing their spouses suddenly realize—just in time—that they've made the wrong decision and decide to remain married.

Amid these hardships, you've changed your mind many times. Some days you thought you'd end up watching certain TV shows, but began other activities. Perhaps people invited you to participate in functions, taking you away from previous plans.

For the moment, financial woes might seem like the biggest, most horrible thing the world has ever known. Tomorrow, or next week, or many years from now, terrorists—now rarely on the minds of many Americans—might succeed in causing widespread damage to a single area or to a wide region.

The Chernobyl nuclear power plant accident of 1986 in Russia still strikes fear in the hearts of many. Nuclear contamination has forced officials to block the general public from visiting that area for hundreds or thousands of years. But because things change, that area will reopen for sure in about 10,000 years—if people are still around.

To many, such knowledge might not be considered a comfort now. Yet nothing of earthly substance lasts forever, just as any negative thoughts in your mind will subside if you let them. The trick is to know and believe attitude changes can and do happen. Several basic changes are helpful in achieving guidance.

To get rid of all Americans, terrorists would have to kill more than 300 million people. Consider that a formidable task that never will be accomplished, since we simply won't permit such destruction. Our collective minds are too powerful, and our hopes and dreams are too great, for us to permit anyone so ruthless—especially terrorists—to rule our world.

"It's not the miles and miles ahead that discourage me, it's the grain of sand in my shoe," as the old saying goes. By overcoming just the smallest of doubts about fear, we can go a long way toward emotional and physical victory.

In this spirit, approach the following belief lessons with an open mind. Carefully undergo painless, step-by-step exercise and delve into widely accepted forms of thought management. What the late TV producer Rod Sterling may have considered as an inescapable "Twilight Zone" gets replaced by mental images of Gene Roddenberry's "Star Trek"—

where you dare to allow your mind to go "where no man has gone before." What at the start seems like a lonely journey can become a pleasure trip.

Enjoy the ride.

Envision a River of Peace

"Testing, one, two, three," the phrase goes, as musicians, recording producers and disc jockeys test their microphones. "Testing, one, two, three." Many of us have heard this phrase on occasion throughout our lifetimes. Most folks never seem to know how this phrase was developed. Yet they instinctively know its cadence.

Last night when you went to sleep, and this morning when you awakened, your brain stayed on overdrive. The thought process never stops, at least from the human perspective. Inner chatter seems continual, more reliable than butterflies that return to Capistrano each year. Mind chatter seems incessant. Endless.

If you're an adult now, imagine what it would be like to live an entire day at your stage in life—all while listening to the exact thought process you had during a 24-hour period as a teen-ager. Needless to say, priorities, worries, concerns and preferences would have changed although the basic personality might stay.

Arguably the best counselors are those who listen with solemn intensity. The ability to listen can result in the proper processing of information. Yet too much data, coming in far too fast might tend to confuse even the most seasoned friends, companions, physicians and even enemies.

Such understanding makes it clear the thought process can be either a hindrance or helpful. The key is to have the "right" thoughts, at appropriate times. Until now you might have thought you had little ability to control your consciousness. Yet these examples are among those considered most effective.

Some have been used for thousands of years, getting very little publicity or widespread recognition. Others might ring a bell, sparking reminders as you see them here. Practice most or all of these exercise, as you begin to discover the power of your brain:

Finger snaps: Prove to yourself fast that you can control your thoughts in an instant. First, snap your fingers once. The second you do that, think of the word "light" and with your eyes closed generate visions of brightness in your mind. Wait a few moments and snap your fingers again. Each time you do this, say "light" and envision brilliance—like the shining of a candle or the sparkle of a light bulb.

After doing this awhile, pause a minute. Then, snap your fingers again saying "dark." With your eyes closed, let your mind generate visions of darkness. After a few moments, do it again: "Dark!" Keep envisioning darkness as you do this. Continue this snap-dark exercise for about five minutes. Already, you realize the power of your mind and its ability to envision.

Now, after a brief break, slowly alternate your snaps. At the start, the second you snap your fingers, create brilliant light in your head. Wait awhile, snap your fingers and do "Dark!" Already, you can see this exercise is more than merely interesting. It can be fun. And it works, especially for those who practice.

Vocalize: When you're alone, say this aloud: "I would love to eat one cookie." As you speak, mean what you say, and envision such food, the most delicious cookies you've ever enjoyed. Allow yourself to get a bit hungry with this sensation. Say it again, "I would love to eat a cookie!" After a few minutes, you might realize you indeed would enjoy eating a single cookie.

Continue this vocalization, but this time say, "I'm full." React as if you would after eating a huge meal. Say it aloud again, repeating, "I'm full." Actualize sensations, and realize you might feel too bloated to eat. The power of your thoughts not only controls the mind, but the body as well.

Quiet talk: Taking the vocalization method a step further, without saying a word, think, "I love not talking." As you think this, consider it a joy to be quiet. Repeat the phrase again, and breathe in slow, "I love not talking." Continue a few minutes, and realize the sensation is real!

Ponder this situation a moment. This time, think, "I wish I had someone to talk to right now." Repeat this phrase mentally, a few moments, "I wish I had someone to talk to right now." After a few minutes of this, you're likely to feel a bit lonely if you *command* yourself to feel that way.

Add values: Either talking or in silence, whichever you prefer, add the injection of "values" to this thought process. This entails such convictions as, "I'm happy when people are good to each other," or "My mind is sharpest in the morning." Think such phrases, tell yourself they're true, and they'll become that in your mind.

The value-adding process is important during the self-enhancement phase as it relates to overcoming fear. Tell yourself whatever you believe under certain circumstances. These are such convictions as "I think greedy corporate lobbyists and misguided politicians who contributed to the economic crisis deserve to be treated such-and-such a way," or "It makes me angry when innocent people get hurt as a result of corporate deregulation allowed by Congress."

Expand possibilities: As you edge into the process of managing fears, realize they never go away even after you've "killed" them. With this understood, expand possibilities of facing your fears by telling yourself you can and will do certain things you've been too fearful to attempt. "I will drive over that bridge tomorrow, although I've been fearful it'll be blown up in a possible terrorist attack."

If tension rattles you as you say this, work through those concerns by attacking them. First, breathe slowly and use relaxation techniques. Then tell yourself, "Other people drive over the bridge, and by golly, I'm going to do it, too." Stretch your mind and your convictions as far as you want within reason. Even if you hadn't thought so before, tell yourself: "It's safe to cross the bridge. I actually believe it's not dangerous. I've changed my mind."

Manage chatter: Remember, it's understandable that everyone's mind is filled with constant chatter. You can and will manage such babble, especially when such thought strike against new convictions and values you've just told yourself. For instance, if your unwanted chatter says, "But I still really am afraid of driving over bridges," change your thoughts by thinking of something pleasant that you enjoy. For instance, if resting on a beach on a sunny summer day is among your favorite activities, put that in your mind as soon as negative thoughts arise. Maybe your mind put up these roadblocks to ban negativity.

Even in the first day of such mind-chatter control management, you're already grasping that such a thought process is not only reasonable and practical—it's possible with persistence and determination. This is not to say you should put yourself in full denial of every potentially bad situation. It just means you're in control when you want.

Open an ant hole: Dubbed "Open An Aunt Hole" for purposes of this exercise, this entails bringing up new possibilities for the first time. The purpose is to begin opening up entirely new value systems. Here are some basics: During some battles, adversaries have tried to get some U.S. prisoners of war to say bad things about America. Patriotic and loyal to their country, most of these captives initially refused to say anything horrible against the USA in front of television cameras or in their writings.

Keen at psychological tactics, captors knew an integral, time-tested way to get prisoners to change. The goal was to start by getting individual Americans to utter just one single bad thing about the United States. Under this strategy, "once an ant is allowed to crawl through a tiny hole, it can reveal an entire colony."

Thus, while feeding prisoners of war, captors strived to engage their inmates in casual chitchat about nothing particularly important. After many months or even years of quiet or non-responses by prisoners, guards might begin to chat about something as "inconsequential" as baseball. "Don't you hate the Dodgers?" a guard might utter in casual conversation.

If after time a prisoner says, "No, I hate the Yankees in New York because they win too much. Other teams should get chances"—the guard secretly becomes victorious because he has opened a proverbial "ant hole." Encouraged by guards who are in full agreement on this issue, the non-important dislike for a baseball team could expand into "I hate the way people in New York talk, their expressions."

All along, the focus by the captors isn't anything particularly about the USA as a whole. Deceptively, the guards bring up numerous other negatives about American society during daily conversations. Trained by their superiors, guards creatively focus conversations on anything and everything negative the prisoner has once said.

After time, the prisoner hears and says only that which is negative. Isolated and lonely, with no outside contact but guards, the prisoner begins to live in a fully negative world, where all thoughts and all discussions are of a "negative nature." And all this contempt began with the suggestion of disliking a baseball team.

If your entire value system is different in some areas than ways you want it to be, you can allow the snap-finger control area of your brain to open up to new possibilities. For instance, if you've always been a pacifist but you're terrified of attacks, you might choose to tell yourself: "It wouldn't hurt if one of those terrorists stubbed his toe. At least that could slow him down a little." By thinking and believing such a scenario is OK and acceptable, the pacifist opens himself up to potential new outcomes and reactions.

Taking this a step further, the same pacifist could consider this notion of toe-stubbing as an "ant hole." There's a chance this thinking could open up new possibilities of thought. *Such a process can change or at least modify an entire value system*.

Adding factors: The same pacifist, who has been fearful, petrified of possibly being injured also can choose to attack his "peace at all costs" attitude. Possible ways to change include adding factors to the thought process, such as "those terrorists kill babies. Look at photographs that I've taped to the refrigerator door of those dead babies. It makes me sick, what those terrorists did. It makes me want to hurt them."

Real objects: The preceding baby photo example underlines the strength of using physical objects in fear management and voluntary mind control. Anyone hoping to generate dislike for our primary enemy could collect dozens of news clippings about its atrocities. These articles could be reread, quoted extensively and *used as propaganda to change the minds of others. A relaxed Mind-Jet pilot realizes "propaganda" occurs and manages it*.

In changing your own mind, you can create internal propaganda. Since your mind is powerful, options are many.

The example of a "pacifist" could be changed around to cover hateful people who strive to become more loving, "unrealistically brave" folks who want to use more caution, and so on. Individual Mind-Jet pilots know such complexities exist. A primary key to happiness is to acknowledge the fact that sadness occurs, and happiness as well. Some believe one of these emotions seemingly couldn't sustain itself without the other, as if each is a necessary opposite.

Cognizant of these diverse mind-management techniques, it's time to actually "kill" your fears. Get ready, because if you want, you're going to create plenty of "dead bodies" in that regard!

Envision a river of peace, guarded by necessary destruction.

Let's roll!

CHAPTER FOURTEEN

3REST™ ~ Day 3 "Careful What You Wish For"

"Be careful what you wish for, because you might get it." It's a phrase many of us have heard and understand full well. For others, such revelations come as new concepts. In life, our dreams for a better future aren't always what they seem.

Statistics reveal a vast majority of lottery winners blow virtually all their winnings within several years. James Dean dreamed of being a movie star. But not long after this actor fulfilled his goal, he died in a car crash that some fans blamed on his "Hollywood" lifestyle.

When confronting economic crisis, we may dream of certain outcomes. But if all our hopes become realities in this case, some people might be sorely disappointed. Hopes of opening new manufacturing facilities might unlock increased immigration problems, squishing some people's dreams of a better life.

And yearning for the best security possible to ward out terrorists might erode certain personal freedoms. Polls show that Americans strongly desire tough national security measures. Yet at the same time many of these same people refuse to relinquish personal liberties they've enjoyed.

Anyone fully determined to kill all their "fears" of terrorism must keep such perspectives in focus. Because the universe mandates change, Mind-Jet pilots from the USA must keep their values on course. Seasoned Mind-Jet pilots know that even when reaching goals, they might lose some things.

How to Eliminate Fear

Forty years before the Attack on America, President John Fitzgerald Kennedy seemed to sum up today's challenge at his inaugural address: "With good conscience our only sure reward, with history the final judge of our deeds, let us go forth to lead the land we love, asking His blessing and His help, but knowing that here on Earth God's work must truly be our own."

Tough decisions each of us makes will reverberate for generations. JFK's revelations have beamed into a present reality, as a torch is passed to a new generation of Americans—tempered by war.

Disciplined by hard times, we struggle for peace through battle. Embracing these truisms seems bittersweet to friend and foe alike. What brings clarity to some also sweeps gloom into the hearts of other people. Such is the stuff, they say, that "dreams are made of."

"There are no winners in war, only losers," polarizes "The price of freedom is justice." It's as if each of us is a child in a playground on a teeter-totter, wondering which side to be on. Yet most of us realize freedom rests on the weighty end.

What this all comes down to as you "kill" your fears of financial strife and terrorism is an unending revelation. Mind-Jet pilots realize their entire earthly goal can and will be swept away by the passage of time. Yet living "in the moment" requires decisive action.

Kill any fears of terrorism and of financial hardship that you desire, realizing all along that the "bodies" of any fear always remain. Sweep through horrors and "just do it." Keep mindful that fears that have been "destroyed" stick around like unwanted cadavers.

Scientists tell us that every action has an opposite reaction. Push something away, and that means it goes somewhere else. This leaves a space, a void that might be filled by someone or something else. For instance, John Doe lived a peaceful life, until a guy named "Harry" terrorized him. Pushed to the edge, John Doe finally killed Harry. The death eliminated Doe's fear of Harry; but now Doe had a new fear—of getting caught.

Life's conflicts between the strong and the weak, the rich and the poor, and so on, trickle through every core of the current worldwide conflict. Just as none of us in the USA is alone in his fears, there are others who are not alone in their collective anger.

Take a universal view. Establish values. Know all along that killing innocent people is "wrong." Humans have an intrinsic right and obligation to protect themselves. These views reflect sensibility, and like it or not justice can and must prevail.

In his "Of Revenge," philosopher Francis Bacon noted that "revenge is kind of wild justice, which the more man's nature runs to, the more ought law to weed it out." Indeed, the "eye-for-an-eye" tactic gets pretty tired when continued for centuries.

In the Appalachian Mountains of the U.S. in the late 19th Century, two families each with at least 13 children battled each other in a curious but legendary feud. It started when one person in the Hatfield family was slain. That led to killings of three McCoys.

Fighting escalated to the point it continued for decades, even after eight combatants were ordered jailed and one got a death sentence. Today, each of us is a "Hatfield." And at the same time, each of us figuratively and literally is a "McCoy."

Anyone who cherishes the sanctity of life and his own "true god" is conflicted. Nonetheless, by killing fears in order to blast through them, you refuse to live a restricted life. Even by remaining "peaceful," you can fight by living free.

President Ronald Reagan, who led the U.S. executive branch of government in the 1980s, spoke of "staying the course." Reagan strived to live and lead as an example, holding a conviction that in order to persevere one must remain on target.

Early this century, before his death, while suffering Alzheimer's, Regan was a "natural victim" of the universe's mandate requiring constant change. Worldwide political changes he helped bring about have been benefiting America since his administration. *Change* that Reagan forced in the Russian government has given the USA a new ally in the terrorism war. *Change* improved technology, enabling U.S. forces to endure more in Afghanistan battles than Soviets had in the 1980s. And *change* in improved media communications enables the American public to understand much more than society did during previous wars.

Yes, *change* is both "bad" and "good." From the perspective of the Taliban terrorist organization, these same developments are negative. "It's a small world after all," as Disney characters love to sing. But in the large scheme of things, there are many diverse and conflicting opinions.

In killing your fears today, program your Mind-Jet to soar above all these "realities." View them as if a disinterested pilot. Realize it's all part of the natural flow of universal joining and pulling apart. You're in control. You're the master of things within your own frame of reference. Delighted is he who savors a morsel of wisdom.

"The dead of midnight is the moon of thought, and midnight mounts her zenith with the stars," Anna Letita Barbauld wrote in "A Summer Evening's Meditation." Sure enough, deep down inside where it counts most, you know what's best for you and for your soul during these challenging times. A humble heart can recognize it's fearful. A humble heart can realize it's OK to be afraid. And even a vengeful heart, or a conceited heart, or a shy heart can blast through and destroy that which is truly evil.

With that understood, here in Day Three of these lessons, take comfort in knowing you can and will kill your fears of terrorism and of economic hardship. You shall pulverize them, those fears you want to eliminate. You shall murder, hang, destroy, whip, annihilate, crucify and chop into little pieces fears caused by any inkling of what you know to be unjust and unfair.

Because you're human, you have a sense of fairness. You can realize and accept the fact "it isn't right" for someone to force you into a lifestyle you don't agree with. So, screw them! To hell with those terrorists! Be gone with the greedy corporate CEOs. Nothing, nothing, nothing can prevent them from making your appointed lifestyle choices, if that's your decision.

Today, if you choose, you can and will make such personal decisions. To wait is to avoid necessary change that will set you free. Truth is setting you free this moment, as you ponder what fear of economic struggle has done to you, your family, friends and co-workers.

It's time to stand up against bullies, just as you stood up against childhood "terrorists" who badgered you in grade school—either through flight or fight. All along, love your enemies, for in their deaths and in the killing of the same fears that these people once instilled in you, they gave you the gift of a stronger life. Without question, you're a "Mighty Mike" inside. And thanks to your moldable mind, you shall overcome. We all shall overcome someday.

Stop the Presses!

"Stop the presses!" yells the war cry. "There's big news this very moment." This term—once a rallying cry for journalists—has become part of our psyches. Americans want results fast.

Our 30-second society demands quick action, from the way we prepare breakfast to how we rush through fast-food lines. This War on Economic Hardship and the War on Terrorism seem to demand urgency in the minds of many. After all, "to act slow might mean death or severe lifelong economic hardship."

Nevertheless, although you're positioned to attack your fears this very moment, it's important to emphasize you're the boss here. You decide when, where and how to work through fears. Refuse to allow lessons or demands from others to dictate such behavior.

What's clear is that to act immediately remains possible. The many 3REST™ examinations you've passed so far clarified your brain's potential. Get comfortable with any progressive behavior if you want, especially peaceful actions from everyday life.

To say this enemy "created my fears" should be crushed or killed, past the point of hate to the eternal essence of mankind. Yes, love!

Hopefully, you're among those who insist it's much better to love than to hate. Even those who are hateful can or should see through the mindless plots of greedy corporations, because destruction never helps us all.

Manage "anger" just as you once allowed fears to manage you. Reverse all hate and dislike for others, even terrorists, knowing your long-term intent is for the greater good. In this sense, you're the "parent," realizing that the best solution is for you to give your various enemies A LOVING DOSE OF HARSH DISCIPLINE.

Buddy System

Thankful that there's "strength in numbers," those of us who share our concerns can find support from others. Those terrified of taking plane trips, for instance, might consider traveling with friends, relatives or co-workers. When that's possible, allow the mind to create a peaceful, powerful and wise imagery companion. Other examples can be helpful:

Distractions: Play a game of solitaire, strike up a conversation with someone, or bring something to read when going into situations that make you anxious. Control your mind in part by bringing it "chatter" other than senseless inner talk that it can generate. Many possibilities abound. Creativity wins.

Parental: Always remember to be your own strong, loving, wise and patient parent. Make a strong inner voice, your reliable guide through fearful situations. Joyful outcomes result. Praise yourself here, still humble to accept what is and what will occur.

Celebrate: Take note of having passed unharmed through situations once thought distressful. Allow your Mind-Jet to breeze above the world's many colorful gardens, at ease with every new triumph.

Universal: Glide through potentially terrible situations, with full realization you're a major part of all creation. Terrorism or corporate greed might sadden you, but you're still capable of focusing on the light of a much greater whole.

Self-appreciation: Acknowledge advances, although in some areas you still might choose not to proceed. Realizing time "heals all wounds," Mind-Jet pilots sense when to increase speed.

Blame: Moving past any need for anger, avoid wasting needless time blaming others. "What is—is." Acknowledge negatives while breezing past them, simply aware they're there.

Dead fear: At this point, acknowledge fears that you've "killed." Move through them, in order to grasp the fact they're merely carcasses. Such bodies serve as reminders of what you've overcome, can overcome and will overcome.

Reverse negatives: Now blessed with an ability to manage thoughts, decide when to flip certain negatives into positives. Thinking "I'm impatient" can become "It'll happen soon enough." When worrying endlessly about a loved one in the U.S. military at war, reverse such thoughts into "at least I have had this person. I have loved him or her, making us both more fulfilled."

Humor & Games: These benefits seem obvious, often helpful distractions that are good for misdirecting the mind.

Your "Unique" Q&A

Here's a short Question-and-Answer session. Envision yourself as the person giving all answers:

Question: Have you killed some fears within three days?

Answer: Yes.

Question: Are there some fears you wanted to kill but didn't.

Answer: Yes.

Question: Did you spare some fears because you just didn't want to kill them?

Answer: Yes.

Question: Could you kill all your remaining fears:

Answer: Yes.

Question: Could you remain afraid if you wanted to?

Answer: Yes.

Question: Then, the decision on whether to be afraid is up to you?

Answer: Yes.

Question: Your answers are irritating! Is "yes" all you ever say?

Answer: Not unless I decide to say something else. It's up to me! I can and have eliminated all fears I wanted to in as little as three days or less!!

CHAPTER FIFTEEN

A Brief Review

Briefly review the Q&A immediately before this section. Realize all questions and answers summarize the way you are. To deny that's the case would be to deny you're breathing this very moment.

Indeed, you've killed fears in as little as three days!

To say you haven't destroyed some fears would be to say you haven't got any control over your brain function. Sure enough, you've shown control

Now that you're graduating from the 3REST™ Program, keep in mind that even the best students return to "school" now and then for refresher courses. In life you will make mistakes and succeed as well, even in your reactions to danger and extreme adversity.

About the Author

A former editor-on-loan to "USA Today" and an experienced book manuscript ghostwriter, Wayne Rollan Melton has been an entertainment columnist, society columnist and features writer, focusing in part on human behavior issues.

Author's Request

Have you had positive experiences, losing or managing fears after reading this book? As the author prepares for follow-up publications, please snail-mail your positive comments to:

Wayne Rollan Melton
PO Box 8184, Reno, NV 89507-8184

Find fulfillment

For details on other books written or ghostwritten by Wayne Rollan Melton, and information on ways to generate income during stressful economic times, visit FixBay.com